The
Crossings

Circle of
Prayer

The Crossings Circle of Prayer

A Journal for Your Journey

CrossAmerica Books for Crossings Book Club
Garden City, New York

© 2000 on behalf of Crossings Book Club

Published by CrossAmerica™ Books, an imprint of CROSSINGS Book Club,
Box GB, 401 Franklin Avenue, Garden City, New York 11530

CrossAmerica™ Books is pending trademark registration on behalf of
CROSSINGS Book Club

ISBN 0-7394-1141-1

Printed in the United States of America

Unless otherwise noted, all Scripture references are taken from the New International Version.
Copyright 1984 by the International Bible Society.

"Forgiveness" by Philip Yancey is taken from *What's So Amazing About Grace? Study Guide* by Philip
Yancey. Copyright 1998 by Philip Yancey. Used by permission of Zondervan Publishing House.

"Prayer as a Pathway to Intimacy with God" by Joni Eareckson Tada is taken from *Holiness in
Hidden Places* by Joni Eareckson Tada. Copyright 1999 by Joni Eareckson Tada. Used by permission
of J. Countryman.

CONTENTS

KEEPING A RECORD
OF GOD'S FAITHFULNESS
How To Use This Book

Every summer when I was a child, my parents would send me to Word of Life camp, a "sleepaway" camp for kids, located in the Adirondack Mountains of upstate New York. Along with the horseback riding, swimming, team sports, and other typical camp activities, Word of Life incorporated lots of Christian training into each day's routine, including guest speakers, morning and evening devotions, campfire sing-alongs and a host of other events. At the time, I was far more interested in having fun than in learning about God. But looking back on those summers, I am amazed at how much I did learn—and still remember—from those camp experiences.

One day, a guest speaker spoke to us about "memorials to God's faithfulness," a pretty serious topic for a little girl to consider. But I was mesmerized as he talked about the fact that God provided his children with reminders of His love that they could see and touch, from the tablets that held the Ten Commandments to the manna in the wilderness to the rainbow.

The speaker went on to say that it is important for us to have "souvenirs" of God's love that we can take out and look at and hold. Actual *things* that can remind us of times in the past when we needed

God in a special way—and He answered. My first memorial to God's faithfulness was a ballpoint pen. I was seven years old and had "borrowed" my older sister's favorite pen. I took it to our backyard and proceeded to play. (What I was *doing* with it is a total mystery to me now!) By the time I needed to return the pen, I had absolutely no idea where it was. I searched the yard for what felt like hours until at last, defeated, I gave up and prepared to face my sister. Then I remembered: I could pray and ask for God's help. I knelt on the grass and asked God to help me in this crisis. As I opened my eyes, they rested on the ground in front of my knees—and there was the pen.

That pen was my first "memorial" to God's faithfulness. Since then, I've prayed thousands of prayers, and as I've gotten older, the prayers have changed to graver subjects than lost pens—my father's diagnosis of cancer, my aging mother's fading ability to care for herself, an illness that doctors couldn't identify, to name just a few. Often, God's answers haven't been as swift in coming as when I found the pen. But over the years, I have amassed a collection of souvenirs of God's faithfulness, the most recent one being my husband, whom I met after decades of praying for a mate yet remaining single.

We know that God doesn't always say "yes" to our prayers. Yet we also know that He is faithful to His children and responsive to our petitions. We know that there is more to prayer than asking for things.

This book has been designed to help you create a running record of your prayer life, of God's answers to prayers—both "yes" and "no." Sometimes God answers with "I've got something for you that you've never even thought of." This book can help you chronicle your journey, so that you can look back on the year, probably having taken detours and side trips that you'd never anticipated, and point to His faithfulness, whatever His answers may have been.

The Crossings Circle of Prayer is divided into twelve chapters, each beginning with an essay devoted to a specific topic regarding the life of prayer. The authors of these essays were carefully chosen for their depth of insight and the special talents and experiences that they bring to their subject.

After the essay, the pages that follow include places for you to record prayer lists, written prayers, and journal entries of your own, and a number of elements that we hope will help you along the way, including tips from fellow members on lots of different topics that we know are of interest to you. These include everything from ways to pray more effectively to suggestions for better organizing your home and your time. Other features include quotes that we think are especially insightful and helpful, as well as written prayers by forefathers in the faith that give voice to thoughts we may not even have yet conceived of. At the end of each chapter, a suggested reading list provides books that are related to the chapter topic and can help you explore it in greater depth.

The final section of the book is entitled "Answered Prayers," and it offers a place for you to testify in writing to God's faithfulness to you in a specific way. It is, in a way, the capstone of a part of your ongoing journey—a "souvenir."

You can use this book systematically, studying each chapter topic in depth for a month at a time (the suggested reading list is designed to help you choose books that address the topic specifically), or you can read all twelve essays at one time and use the journal as as often as you wish.

Our prayer for you is that *The Crossings Circle of Prayer* will help you add depth and breadth to your journey and then remain for you as a physical reminder of God's work in your life throughout the year.

The Editors

Crossings Book Club

The Tools of Prayer

THE TOOLS OF PRAYER
BY SHARON JEHLEN

Prayer, like so many of the things God blesses us with so richly, is an unmerited privilege—the privilege to go directly before the Father and lay our requests at His feet. But it is not a privilege in the sense that it should be used sparingly; it is absolutely essential for developing intimacy with God.

In the days before telephones and e-mail, people communicated with one another by means of letters. Many people, no doubt, simply wrote informational letters, but the really interesting letters, the ones that have survived and given us a wonderful picture of life in other times, shared the writer's thoughts, feelings, and impressions—they shared the person. Through those letters, the recipient began to know the writer, and in spite of separation of hundreds of miles, intimacy developed.

Great letter writers become that way because they write many, many letters. It is a skill that needs to be developed, and it's the same with prayer. We can exercise the privilege of prayer by repeating the same words daily and by simply asking God to supply our needs, but that's a bit like the college student who writes home only to ask his parents for money. The letter is nice, and it lets the parents know he's at least well enough to hold a pen, but it doesn't let them into his life. In the same way, God does honor those prayers, but He yearns for much more than that. When we open our hearts to God and lay bare our souls to Him, our relationship with Him deepens.

There are many tools available to us that can help us develop our prayer skills. The first and best tool is God's word. From the Psalms to the Lord's Prayer to Paul's letters to the early church, we have countless examples of prayers right in the Bible. There we find God's promises to us that we can claim. But more than that, God's word is His letter to us—it is how we know Him, what He is like, what He desires for us. Without regular study of the Scriptures, prayer is like one-sided correspondence.

Studying the Scriptures can also point out our errors and correct our faults when we pray for wrong things, and give instruction for right praying. When we're harboring resentment, God's word gently reminds us that we're to pray for our enemies. When we pray selfishly, we recall the words of James, "When you ask, you do not receive, because you ask with wrong motives, that you may spend what you get on your pleasures" (James 4:3).

The second tool that we can use is the body of Christ, the church. It was never God's intention that we should worship Him in solitude. After God created Adam, He said, "It is not good that man should be alone" (Gen. 2:18). Jesus promised, "Where two or three are gathered in my name, there am I in the midst of them" (Matt. 18:20). Paul exhorted the Galatians, "Bear one another's burdens" (Gal. 6:2). Praying with one another, praying for one another, and even discussing what we pray about with other believers can deepen our relationship with God.

Several years ago, my husband received a promotional sample of an electronic Bible. It would have been a nice thing to keep because it would have been a great tool for our own Bible study. But my husband thought our friend Norm would really enjoy it, so we decided to give it to him. The next time we saw Norm, we gave it to him, and he was overwhelmed. He told us that he had really wanted an electronic Bible, and he had been praying about whether he should purchase one for himself.

That incident has stayed with me, because it taught me a good deal about prayer. Norm wanted this thing and consulted God about whether he should purchase it. Now there is no question that an electronic Bible is a good thing, and there is no reason God would not want Norm to have it. If Norm had simply bought the Bible because it was a good thing to have, though, all of us would have missed out on God's blessing of using us to answer his prayer. It is absolutely staggering to think that God cares about something as small as whether our friend purchased an electronic Bible. But even more than that, He knew that by answering Norm's prayer in that way, our hearts would be blessed as well, and we would be encouraged.

Aside from those two very broad tools, there are several specific things we can do to sharpen our praying skills. Simple things, like praying the "ACTS" model—adoration, confession, thanksgiving, supplication—help us to focus our prayers and give them balance. Often I want to go straight to the supplication part, but having that little tool handy makes me stop and worship first.

Although it might sound rigid and lacking in spontaneity, it helps to have a little structure in your prayers. For example, devote your prayers on Monday to your husband and your marriage; on Tuesday, pray for members of your immediate family; Wednesday, pray for your friends' prayer needs; Thursday, remember the requests that were mentioned at Wednesday night prayer meeting; and so on.

Praying in a group and listening to what other people pray for and how they pray can be a precious experience. There is nothing like it for really getting a glimpse into another person's heart. One person talks to God very naturally, clearly in conversation with a loving Father; another may be nakedly honest, knowing that nothing can be hidden from God. Other people approach God in different ways than I do, and by listening to their prayers I learn from them.

Throughout history believers have left us with a rich legacy of their prayers, many of which have been written down. These also teach us by their varied ways of talking to God, but they do more than that. When our prayers are dry, we can borrow the words of Martin Luther, Amy Carmichael, Dietrich Bonhoeffer, and others to express the needs of our hearts.

Whether it's simply a log of prayer requests and answers, or a more intimate record of your actual prayers, keeping a journal is another effective tool in becoming a practiced prayer warrior. When you're experiencing times of doubt, it's wonderful to look back and see specifically the ways God has demonstrated His faithfulness and sovereignty.

Finally, there are scores and scores of books written about prayer, about becoming intimate with God, and about the nature and character of God. These books can broaden your knowledge and deepen your understanding of the privilege God has extended to you, as His child, to come to Him in prayer.

15

No matter how many books you read, though, or how eloquent your journal entries are, remember that the important thing is simply to pray. Someone once said, "God doesn't have favorites, but he does have intimates." What a concept! As you reflect on this, I encourage you to let your "spiritual correspondence" with God be such that you become one of God's intimates.

SHARON JEHLEN *is manager of publications for Women of Faith, and is the former editor for Crossings for Kids Book Club. Her current writing projects include two novels and a devotional hymn book for children.*

*Pray this month with
Crossings for each
of us to gain a spiritual
friend and mentor, who
will strengthen and stand
with us in our efforts to
follow Christ.*

Psalm 42:7 reads "Deep calls to deep." Perhaps somewhere in the subterranean chambers of your life you have heard the call to deeper, fuller living. You have become weary of frothy experiences and shallow teaching. Every now and then you have caught glimpses, hints of something more than you have known.

—Richard Foster

After Christmas and other holidays I take advantage of the sales where I save 50 to 75%. I buy gifts, gift wrap, cards, and decorations. I also watch for other sales through the year where I find bargains that I can add to my gift box. When a birthday, anniversary, wedding, baby shower, or holiday comes along and I need a gift, I don't have to take time to go shopping; I just go to my gift box. When holidays come and it is time to decorate, I often have plenty to decorate with from the sale items I purchased after the previous holiday. These ideas not only save time and keep the tension level low, but they also save me money.

—Betty Skerbitz, Tulsa, Oklahoma
Crossings member

19

_____

_____

_____

_____

_____

_____

_____

_____

_____

_____

ꝏ

God is our home, but many of us have strayed from our native land.
—Archbishop Desmond Tutu

Member To Member

After the new year I take all my Christmas cards and keep them near my Bible reading area. Each week I choose a card and pray for that family all week long. Then I write a note on the back of the picture part of the card and drop it in the mail like a postcard.

—Penny J. Roberts, Seaside, California
Crossings member

Lord, forgive me that I have so little time to spend on my knees.
Raising children and running a busy house,
I have to do most of my praying "on the hoof," as it were.
But, Lord, You know my heart is kneeling.

—Ruth Bell Graham

Write a letter to God about your life. What would you like to see happen in the next three to six months? What would you like to learn about God? How would you like to change or grow? What requests would you like answered?…Write out your feelings, goals, and requests…. Place it in a prominent place, like your Bible, with a date written on the outside, then open it on that date.

—Pam Farrel

ॐ

Scripture is like a river, broad and deep, shallow enough here for the lamb to go wading, but deep enough there for the elephant to swim.

—Gregory the Great

Member To Member

After examining my prayer life, I realized I needed to praise the Lord more than I was. I began to praise God for all the wonderful ways he had answered my prayers in the past and to recognize all the blessings he has given me that were not answered prayers. These blessings include everything from the artistry of a hummingbird to the lopsided smile my son has. My feet never touch the ground in the morning that I do not thank God for the blessing of this day He has given me.

—Karen Koenig, Buckner, Arkansas
Crossings member

❧

If there are any tears shed in heaven, they will be over the fact that we prayed so little.

—Billy Graham

Another year is dawning:
Dear Father, let it be,
In working or in waiting,
Another year with Thee;
Another year of progress,
Another year of praise,
Another year of proving
Thy presence all the days.

Another year of mercies,
Of faithfulness and grace;
Another year of gladness
In the shining of Thy face;
Another year of leaning
Upon Thy loving breast;
Another year of trusting,
Of quiet, happy rest.
—Frances Ridley Havergal

> God didn't design prayer so that you would get better, even though you will. God didn't design prayer so you would be holy, even though that does happen…. God designed prayer—and get this straight before we go any further—because he likes you and wants to spend time with you.
> —Steve Brown

_____

❧

The purpose of prayer is not to inform God of our needs, but to invite Him to rule our lives.
—Clarence Bauman

_____

_____

_____

_____

_____

_____

_____

_____

Never say *you will pray about a thing;* pray about it. *Our Lord's teaching about prayer is so amazingly simple but at the same time so amazingly profound that we are apt to miss his meaning. The danger is to water down what Jesus says about prayer and make it mean something more common sense; if it were only common sense, it was not worth His while to say it. The things Jesus says about prayer are supernatural revelations. "For your Father knows the things you have need of before you ask Him." If God sees that my spiritual life will be furthered by giving the things for which I ask, then He will give them, but that is not the end of prayer. The end of prayer is that I come to know God Himself.*

—Oswald Chambers

*Let nothing disturb you,
    nothing alarm you:
while all things fade away
God is unchanging.
Be patient
and you will gain everything:
for with God in your heart
nothing is lacking,
God meets your every need.*
            —St. Teresa of Avila

ॐ

It is a good thing to let prayer be the first business of the morning and the last of the evening.
            —Martin Luther

Member To Member

My best friend, Vi Anderson, and I have celebrated our friendship with communion. We have shared the symbols of the covenant at our kitchen tables. We celebrate friendship in Him and with Him—our very best friend.

—Earlin Hansen, Ferndale, Washington
Crossings member

27

Jesus taught us that we might pray for personal benefits and protection, but it is not recorded that He did so. Perhaps one reason our prayer life is so fruitless is that it mainly consists of requests for things to help us rather than what would glorify God.

—Fred Fisher

> *Prayer is not so much the means whereby God's will is bent to man's desires. The real end of prayer is not so much to get this or that single desire granted, as to put human life into full and joyful conformity with the will of God.*
>
> —Charles Brent

_____

_____

_____

_____

_____

_____

_____

_____

_____

_____

_____

_____

_____

ॐ

God insists that we ask, not because He needs to know our situation, but because we need the spiritual discipline of asking.

—Catherine Marshall

Reading List

30 Ways to Wake Up Your Quiet Time, Pam Farrel, InterVarsity Press

The Art of Prayer, Timothy Jones, Doubleday

A Journey Into Prayer, Evelyn Christenson, Victor Books

A Method for Prayer, Matthew Henry, Christian Focus Publications

The Imitation of Christ, Thomas à Kempis, Image Books

Prayer, O. Hallesby, Augsburg Fortress Publishers

Prayer, Richard Foster, HarperCollins Publishers

Prayer Can Change Your Life, Becky Tirabissi, Thomas Nelson Publishers

Self-Abandonment to Divine Providence, Jean-Pierre de Caussade, Tan Books & Publishers

A Woman's Walk With God, Sheila Cragg, Crossway Books

On Worship

On Worship
by Joel Belz

Is it overly forward, or too informal, to think of worship as a conversation with God? Not if He says that's what it is.

This is no mere chitchat, you understand—and by no means the conversation of equals. But it's a conversation, nonetheless. And so some basic rules of conversation apply.

A key element of any good conversation is that there be some balance, some genuine give and take. Believe it or not, true worship—even the worship of the great Creator God—also includes a certain symmetry and proportion. There's a time to talk, and a time to listen.

That's why throughout the history of God's people, there has been something we call "liturgy." There's formal liturgy and informal liturgy. There's liturgy when you gather with the rest of God's people for worship, but there's also liturgy when you worship God all by yourself. Liturgy provides a framework for the conversation between God and His people. Liturgy keeps the conversation from wandering—but it's also there to keep the conversation from getting lopsided, one way or the other.

Not that it would be wrong if the conversation got lopsided in God's favor. He has every right to dominate any discussion between Himself and His people. The wonder is that He chooses to let us talk to Him at all. Indeed, the Bible suggests He even delights to hear us talk. But given that wonderful privilege, how dare we even think of doing it the wrong way?

Especially considering the status of the One we're talking to, we're wise to learn and then to keep in mind a few of the applicable ground rules.

For example, it's basic in conversation to avoid self-centeredness, but instead to steer the focus toward things that are interesting to the person you're talking to. With the God we pray to, there are things we know are of enormous interest to Him.

Strange as it may sound, one of the subjects God is most interested in is Himself! To the very extent that we find it hard to understand such a concept, we demonstrate how vastly we underestimate the greatness of the God we worship. We keep measuring Him by our own standards. But the very fact that He is great enough and good enough to want our attention and adoration—that's why He's great enough and good enough to worship!

And no, we're not just trying to manipulate God. If He's as great and as good as we say, we'll never do that in any case. He is (and this is greatly to our advantage) an enormous topic for discussion. When we choose to focus on Him, we won't run out of things to say anytime soon. There will be no embarrassing blank spots in the conversation where we'll be tempted to change the subject. God and all of His works are big enough to fill our thoughts for the rest of eternity.

So you should become an imitator of David in the Psalms. Part of the time, you'll just talk about the incredible character of God, and all His attributes. Part of the time, you'll marvel out loud about His creation. And then, of course, you'll also talk to God about the specifics of His love and His care for His people—including you. In all that, you'll be conversing with God about His very favorite subject: Himself.

But wonder of wonders, this great God—this vast and infinite person we worship—is also interested in other subjects as well. According to His own word, He's also interested in you and me, as individuals, with all our idiosyncrasies and problems and failures and heartaches. He's interested in us even with our deliberate sin and rebellion against Him. He invites us—no, He even commands us—to come and talk to Him about all those intensely personal matters.

Here, too, we can imitate David in the Psalms, where it is not hard to find lengthy passages of self-reflection. There's no need for embarrassment when we shift the focus from time to time from God to us. God understands that shift; it's just fine, for He also understands that the shift itself will ultimately chase us right back to Himself.

JOEL BELZ *is the publisher of* World Magazine, *and a contributing author to* Whirled Views: Tracking Today's Culture Storms *(Crossway Books).*

*P*ray for schoolteachers
and administrators, that they
would approach their work
with humility, patience, and
a true passion for teaching.

35

Praise to the Lord, the Almighty, the King of creation!
O my soul, praise Him, for He is thy health and salvation!
All ye who hear, now to His temple draw near;
Join me in glad adoration!

Praise to the Lord, who o'er all things so wondrously reigneth,
Shelters thee under His wings, yea, so gently sustaineth!
Hast thou not seen how thy desires e'er have been
Granted in what He ordaineth?

—Joachim Neander

❧

The most valuable thing the Psalms do for me is to express that same delight in God which made David dance.

—C.S. Lewis

Member To Member

If you time a household task, for instance how long it takes to unload the dishwasher or fold a load of clothes, you'll be surprised how little time it takes and you won't put it off because you only have fifteen minutes.

—Judy Schmidt, Arapaho, Oklahoma
Crossings member

I will praise You, O Lord, with my whole heart; I will tell of all Your marvelous works. I will be glad and rejoice in You: I will sing praise to Your name, O Most High.

—Ps. 9:1–2

The night before our family events, we pack the car with the supplies we will need, so we don't feel rushed the next day.

—Shirley Walker, Sparta, Wisconsin
Crossings member

38

*I awoke heavy
and heavy I prayed,
face in the sun,
heart in the shade.
As smoke hangs low
on a sullen day,
my prayer hung there...
till I heard His voice,
"This is the day
that the Lord hath made";
Rejoice!*

—Ruth Bell Graham

Whether it's a financial crunch, a sudden illness, or a personal defeat, if you fix your heart on praise to God, then you have offered a sacrifice. If you've ever cried during those heartbreaking difficulties, "Lord, I will hope in You and praise You more and more," then you know you have offered words that have cost you plenty. Praise in those circumstances is painful.... Please remember this: Most of the verses written about praise in God's Word were voiced by people faced with crushing heartaches...they knew that the sacrifice of praise was a key to victory on their spiritual journey.
—Joni Eareckson Tada

39

_____

⤳

*So many things will offer themselves for "worship" today.
But reveal yourself, God, in all your creativity, as the
only Being worthy of my true adoration.*
—Gary Wilde

> *Once you have called out to Him, you can lift up your hands in praise. No matter what you have suffered, you can hold up your head. Regardless of who has hurt you, hold up your head! Put aside those who mistreated you....You can't change where you have been, but you can change where you are going.*
>
> —T.D. Jakes

❦

> *God specializes in things fresh and firsthand. His plans for you this year may outshine those of the past.... He's prepared to fill your days with reasons to give Him praise.*
>
> —Joni Eareckson Tada

Member To Member

I've taken to singing the praise songs used both in my church services and children's Sunday school. Repetitious, yes, but they get my mind God-centered and get me outside myself. I'm better able to pray for others, to pray for bigger issues: our nation, the world's children, etc.

—Gail Stoltzfoos, Gordonville, Pennsylvania
Crossings member

When we are caught up in the celebration of God there is neither room nor time for the invasion of negative living. As we rejoice before the Lord, as we serve Him in the area of our calling, as we enter into the love that surrounds our days, as we give thanks to Him for His kindness and faithfulness, we celebrate God.

—Luci Swindoll

> *Let us therefore desire nothing else, wish for nothing else, and let nothing please and delight us except our Creator and Redeemer, and Savior, the only true God, who is full of good, who alone is good, merciful and kind, gentle and sweet, who alone is holy, just, true, and upright, who alone is benign, pure and clean, from whom, and through whom, and in whom is all mercy, all grace, all glory of all penitents and of the just, and of all the blessed rejoicing in heaven. Let nothing therefore hinder us, let nothing separate us, let nothing come between us.*
>
> —St. Francis of Assisi

ๅ

God's goodness hath been great to thee. Let never day nor night unhallowed pass but still remember what the Lord hath done.
—William Shakespeare

Member To Member

Occasionally I will write my prayer for a person down and mail it to the friend I prayed for. Someone did this for me, and it arrived at exactly the time I needed a reminder of God's love for me.

—Beth Bakken, Pullman, Washington
Crossings member

43

The act of worship internalizes the way of discipleship into habits of praise and obedience so that life is not a depressing descent into senility, but an exhilarating ascent to strength.

—Eugene Peterson

> When you recognize God
> as Creator, you will admire
> Him. When you recognize
> His wisdom, you will learn
> from Him. When you discover
> His strength, you will rely on
> Him. But only when He saves
> you will you worship Him.
> —Max Lucado

᷈

Even in the dark times, we must realize the vast power of worship to give our lives meaning and purpose.

—Jack Hayford

Reading List

Fix Your Eyes on Jesus, Anne Ortlund, Word Publishing

A Gathering of Hope, Helen Hayes, Walker & Co.

In His Steps, Charles Sheldon, Barbour Publishing

A Lifestyle of Worship, David Morris, Regal Books

A Long Obedience in the Same Direction, Eugene Peterson,
    InterVarsity Press

The One Year Book of Hymns, edited by Robert K. Brown, Tyndale
    House Publishers

The Practice of the Presence of God, Brother Lawrence, Fleming H.
    Revell Co.

Prayers from the Heart, Richard Foster, Harper San Francisco

The Pursuit of God, A.W. Tozer, Christian Publications

Spiritual Moments with the Great Hymns, Evelyn Bence,
    Zondervan Publishing House

The Vision of His Glory, Anne Graham Lotz, Word Publishing

Venite: A Book of Daily Prayer, Robert Benson, Tarcher/Putnam

Widening
Your Circle of Influence
Through Prayer

❧ **MARCH** ❧

WIDENING YOUR CIRCLE OF INFLUENCE THROUGH PRAYER
BY STORMIE OMARTIAN

How can I possibly make a difference in this world? I'm just one person!
I see so many things happening around me that I am concerned about,
but what can I do to bring about any kind of positive change? What is
the most effective way for me to contribute something good to the lives
of the people I care about?

We've all asked ourselves questions like that at one time or another,
especially when we see need and feel powerless to meet it. But the answer
to each one of these questions is simple: we can pray. Through prayer
we are able to touch the world around us in far greater depth than we
ever dreamed possible. Our problem is that we are often shortsighted
in our praying.

Most of us are not reticent to pray for our own needs and concerns.
Nor should we be. After all, Jesus said there are things we lack in our lives
because we do not ask God for them. Yet we frequently stop there and
venture no further. We fail to see the impact of our prayers when they
reach out to an ever-widening circle around ourselves. We don't recognize
our own potential for influence.

The best place to start as an intercessor (one who pleads with God on
behalf of another) is to pray first for the ones closest to us—our husbands,
wives, children, mothers, fathers, brothers, sisters, nieces, and nephews.

What happens to them affects our lives too. Their sorrow is our sorrow. Their joy is ours as well. From these we can move into prayer for our extended family members, friends, neighbors, people in our community, leaders in our state and nation, and ultimately people and situations we are aware of around the world. But we often stop praying long before we ever get that far because we believe that the world is too big for our tiny prayers to make much of a difference. And that's true if we merely look at the situation from our own perspective. Our prayers are tiny. Our solitary voice is weak. But when we see things from God's perspective, we understand that although our prayers may be small in relation to problems in the world around us, our God is big. Nothing is impossible for Him.

With God, there are no time or space limitations. That means we can pray for someone on the other side of the world, and our prayers will be just as powerful as if that person were sitting right next to us. We can pray about things before they happen. Can there be any doubt that prayer played an important part in bringing the crew of Apollo 13 home safely after an explosion on board their space ship as they traveled on their mission to the moon? This is not to minimize what the brilliant people of the NASA space program did to bring these men home safely. One tiny miscalculation or human error and the crew would have perished. But the astronauts' situation was precarious and extremely life threatening and what they had to do to get home had never even been tried before. They had no guarantees. There can be no doubt that the prayers of countless believers on earth, both before and during the crisis, helped save the lives of three brave men thousands of miles into space.

Whether we pray for someone across the table, across the room, across the country, on the far side of our planet, or on the other side of the moon, our prayers are powerfully far-reaching. That's because when we draw near to God, He draws near to us. When we call upon the Lord, He hears and answers.

The point of all this is to encourage you to think of yourself as a person who is able to profoundly affect the world around you. The less you underestimate the power of your prayers, the greater their impact will be. In fact, your sphere of influence will be as broad as your prayer list is long.

STORMIE OMARTIAN *is a best-selling author of several books, including her autobiography,* Stormie, *and the Gold-Medallion nominated* The Power of a Praying Wife. *She was contributing editor for* Virtue Magazine *and* Total Health, *and is a popular conference speaker on the subject of the power of prayer.*

This month, pray with Crossings for local organizations and ministries that provide help to others in your area. Pray for wisdom in the use of their time and finances, and pray for more volunteers.

51

_____

_____

_____

_____

_____

_____

_____

_____

_____

_____

_____

_____

_____

_____

_____

_____

_____

— Member To Member —

I have found it is most helpful to set up a "housework schedule."
I do two or three chores every evening after getting home from work:
Monday—do laundry, change bedding; Tuesday—vacuum and dust, etc.
In this way, by Friday or Saturday, my house is clean and I have the
weekend free to do what I wish.

—Mary Jones, Gadsden, Alabama
Crossings member

_____

_____

_____

_____

_____

_____

_____

We commend to your care all those who find life too much for them;
those who daily have to face jobs with which they cannot cope;
those who are daunted by the whole business of living;
those whose families make demands on them which they cannot meet;
those who cannot summon up the strength to do the things they
*   know have to be done;*
those who feel they cannot go on.
Lord, giver of life, give them life.

—from *Further Everyday Prayers*

> ...[A]ll of the churches across the land are filled with people praying and singing, but why is it that there is so little improvement, so few results from so many prayers? The reason is none other than the one which James speaks of when he says, "You ask and do not receive because you ask amiss" (James 4:3). For where this faith and confidence is not in the prayer, the prayer is dead.
>
> —Martin Luther

๛

Men may spurn our appeals, reject our message, oppose our arguments, despise our persons, but they are helpless against our prayers.

—Sidlow Baxter

Christ for the world we sing;
The world to Christ we bring
With loving zeal—
The poor and them that mourn,
The faint and overborne,
Sin-sick and sorrow-worn,
For Christ to heal.

Christ for the world we sing;
The world to Christ we bring
With fervent prayer—
The wayward and the lost,
By restless passions tossed,
Redeemed at countless cost
From dark despair.
—Samuel Wolcott

54

Member To Member

I keep a prayer journal for my friends or anyone I feel led to pray for. When the journals are full, I give them to the person as a gift. The idea has grown so that I now usually have at least three journals I'm writing for others plus mine.

—Kathy Thorbjornsen, Chesapeake, Virginia
Crossings member

As Christians we are justified in being angry with evil. But with anger goes the responsibility of compassionately loving those whom evil is destroying and giving of ourselves to fight the evil.

—Chip Ricks

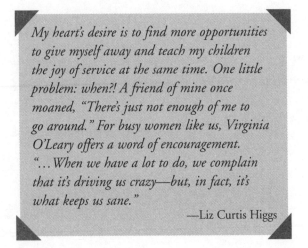

My heart's desire is to find more opportunities to give myself away and teach my children the joy of service at the same time. One little problem: when?! A friend of mine once moaned, "There's just not enough of me to go around." For busy women like us, Virginia O'Leary offers a word of encouragement. "...When we have a lot to do, we complain that it's driving us crazy—but, in fact, it's what keeps us sane."

—Liz Curtis Higgs

_____

_____

_____

_____

_____

_____

> *God of all the nations of the earth, remember the multitudes who, though created in Your image, have not known You, nor the dying of Your Son their Savior Jesus Christ. Grant that by the prayers and work of Your holy church they may be delivered from all ignorance and unbelief and brought to worship You; through Him whom You have sent to be the resurrection and the life of all people, your Son Jesus Christ our Lord.*
>
> —St. Francis Xavier

57

_____

_____

_____

_____

_____

_____

_____

ᔰ

Those who quietly, through prayer, used God's power, were the ones who made the world move forward.

—Edward P. Roe

Member To Member

I've traveled and worked with my husband, and our long days started early. One morning the Holy Spirit impressed me with the following, which can be creatively prayed as brief or lengthy.

S (Sunday)—pray for sermons, songs, and Sunday schools
M (Monday)—pray for men, as individuals, husbands, fathers, and so on
T (Tuesday)—pray for tiny tots to teens to twenties and thirties
W (Wednesday)—pray for women, as individuals, wives, mothers, and so on
T (Thursday)—pray for teachers and mentors
F (Friday)—pray for families
S (Saturday)—pray for salvation and growth

—Shirley Hackett, Falls City, Nebraska
Crossings member

In Ephesians 6:10–20, the whole point is that the "armor of God" is
needed to stand against, to wrestle against the "wiles of the devil." And
it is there, in that context, that we are commanded to "pray always with
all prayer and supplication in the Spirit." Prayer is not just icing on the
cake of a so-called spiritual life; prayer is warm, close communication
with the living God, and also a matter of doing an active work on
His side of the battle.

—Edith Schaeffer

_____

_____

_____

_____

_____

_____

_____

_____

_____

_____

_____

_____

_____

_____

⌇

*In praying for people one dislikes I find it helpful to remember that one
is joining in* His *prayer for them.*

—C.S. Lewis

Part of the Spirit's gift is discernment. If we are to pray for ourselves and others according to the mind of Christ, we need to be led by the Spirit to know what to pray for and how and when. Jesus, too, had to pray for discernment; His mind was subjected to the Spirit, not automatically, but through prayer. He needed to soak Himself in the Father's presence and sensitize Himself to the Father's will.

—Maria Boulding

60

ॐ

There is nothing that makes us love a man so much as praying for him.

—William Law

Reading List

Becoming a Prayer Warrior, Elizabeth Alves, Gospel Light Publications

Beyond Ourselves, Catherine Marshall, Fleming H. Revell Co.

Fresh Wind, Fresh Fire, Jim Cymbala, Zondervan Publishing House

Intercessory Prayer, Dutch Sheets, Regal Books

Jesus Freaks, DC Talk and Voice of the Martyrs, Albury Publishing

Joshua, Joseph Girzone, Doubleday

Out of the Salt Shaker and into the World, Rebecca Manley Pippert, Intervarsity Press

The Power of a Praying Wife, Stormie Omartian, Harvest House Publishers

Prayers That Avail Much, Word Ministries, Harrison House Publishers

Praying for the World's 365 Most Influential People, David Kopp, Harvest House Publishers

The Secret of Intercession, Andrew Murray, Whitaker House

The Seven Storey Mountain, Thomas Merton, Harcourt Brace

This Present Darkness, Frank Peretti, Crossway Books

Through Gates of Splendor, Elisabeth Eliot, Tyndale House Publishers

Forgiveness

FORGIVENESS
BY PHILIP YANCEY

In the heat of an argument, my wife came up with an acute theological formulation. We were discussing my shortcomings in a rather spirited way when she said, "I think it's pretty amazing that I forgive you for some of the dastardly things you've done!"

Since I'm writing about forgiveness, not sin, I will omit the juicy details of those dastardly things. What struck me about her comment, rather, was its sharp insight into the nature of forgiveness. Forgiveness is an unnatural act—my wife expressed this truth as if by instinct. The very taste of forgiveness seems somehow wrong. Even when we have committed a wrong, we want to earn our way back into the injured party's good graces. We prefer to crawl on our knees, to wallow, to do penance, to kill a lamb—and religion often obliges us.

Yet Jesus instructed us to (pray), "Forgive us our trespasses, as we forgive those who trespass against us." At the center of the Lord's Prayer, which Jesus taught us to recite, lurks the unnatural act of forgiveness. Jesus hinged God's forgiveness on our willingness to forgive unjust acts.

Theologically, the Gospels give a straightforward answer to why God asks us to forgive: because that is what God is like. When Jesus first gave the command, "Love your enemies," He added this rationale: "…that you may be sons of your Father in heaven. He causes His sun to rise in the evil and the good, and sends rain on the righteous and the unrighteous."

✿ Forgiveness ✿

The Gospel of grace begins and ends with forgiveness. And people write songs with titles like "Amazing Grace" for one reason: Grace is the only force in the universe powerful enough to break the chains that enslave generations. Grace alone melts ungrace.

Forgiveness alone can halt the cycle of blame and pain, breaking the cycle of ungrace. It does not settle all questions of blame and fairness— often it pointedly evades those questions—but it does allow a relationship to start over, to begin anew. In that way, said Solzhenitsyn, we differ from all animals. Not our capacity to think, but our capacity to repent and to forgive makes us different. Only humans can perform that most unnatural act, which transcends the relentless law of nature.

If we do not transcend nature, we remain bound to the people we cannot forgive, held in their vise grip. This principle applies even when one party is wholly innocent and the other wholly to blame, for the innocent party will bear the wound until he or she can find a way to release it—and forgiveness is the only way.

The second great power of forgiveness is that it can loosen the stranglehold of guilt in the perpetrator. Magnanimous forgiveness allows the possibility of transformation in the guilty party.

Forgiveness—undeserved, unearned—can cut the cords and let the oppressive burden of guilt roll away. The New Testament shows a resurrected Jesus leading Peter by the hand through a threefold ritual of forgiveness. Peter need not go through life with the guilty, hangdog look of one who had betrayed the Son of God. Oh, no. On the backs of such transformed sinners Christ would build His church.

God shattered the inexorable law of sin and retribution by invading earth, absorbing the worst we had to offer, crucifixion, and then fashioning from that cruel deed the remedy for the human condition. Calvary broke up the logjam between justice and forgiveness. By accepting onto His innocent self all the severe demand of justice, Jesus broke forever the chain of ungrace.

One day I discovered this admonition from the apostle Paul tucked in among many other admonitions in Rom. 12. Hate evil, Be joyful, Live in harmony, Do not be conceited—the list goes on and on. Then appears this verse, "Do not take revenge, my friends, but leave room for God's wrath, for it is written: 'It is mine to avenge; I will repay,' says the Lord."

At last I understood: In the final analysis, forgiveness is an act of faith. By forgiving another, I am trusting that God is a better justice-maker than I am. By forgiving, I release my own right to get even and leave all issues of fairness for God to work out. I leave in God's hands the scales that must balance justice and mercy.

I never find forgiveness easy, and rarely do I find it completely satisfying. Nagging injustices remain, and the wounds still cause pain. I have to approach God again and again, yielding to Him the residue of what I thought I had committed to Him long ago. I do so because the Gospels make clear the connection: God forgives my debts as I forgive my debtors. The reverse is also true. Only by living in the stream of God's grace will I find the strength to respond with grace toward others.

❦

PHILIP YANCEY *is editor at large for* Christianity Today *magazine, and is the author of more than a dozen books, including two winners of the Gold Medallion Book of the Year:* The Jesus I Never Knew *and* What's So Amazing About Grace?, *from which this essay is taken.*

~ *Forgiveness* ~

*P*ray for prison ministries
as they convey God's love and
forgiveness to inmates
and their families.

67

_____

_____

_____

_____

_____

_____

_____

_____

_____

_____

_____

_____

_____

_____

_____

_____

_____

_____

Lord, make me an instrument of
    thy peace;
where there is hatred, let me sow love;
where there is injury, pardon;
where there is doubt, faith;
where there is despair, hope;
where there is darkness, light;
and where there is sadness, joy.

O Divine Master, grant that I may
    not so much seek
to be consoled as to console,
not so much to be understood as
    to understand,
not so much to be loved as to love;
for it is in giving that we receive,
it is in pardoning that we are
    pardoned,
it is in dying that we awake to
    eternal life.
                    —St. Francis of Assisi

68

☙

To witness the miracle of rivers in the desert, you have to be in the desert.
                                        —Penelope Stokes

In these days we are in training for the kingdom of peace that will come on earth. The Bible is full of promises of things that are going to happen when Jesus returns. The wolf will lie down with the lamb, swords will be changed into plowshares....

Perhaps you say: "Yes, that will be wonderful and then it will be quite easy for me, but now there is nothing but squabbling, criticism, irritation, especially among Christians."

That is true. But especially in this dark world, the Lord Jesus gave us the task of passing on His love.

—Corrie ten Boom

↭

I think that if God forgives us we must forgive ourselves. Otherwise it is almost like setting up ourselves as a higher tribunal than Him.

—C.S. Lewis

We would get on better if we could ignore or dismiss offending people. A private religion would be much more to our taste. But God will not permit it: we must learn God's forgiveness and love among people whom we forgive and love.

—Eugene Peterson

৵
Easter is the New Year's Day of the soul.
—A.B. Simpson

_____

_____

_____

_____

_____

_____

_____

_____

_____

_____

_____

_____

_____

_____

_____

_____

The great Easter truth is not that we are to live newly after death—that is not the great thing—but that we are to be new here and now by the power of the resurrection; not so much that we are to live forever as that we are to, and may, live nobly now because we are to live forever.

—Phillips Brooks

Even in an exceptionally busy week I take time to quickly clean the kitchen and bathroom. If company comes, they may see clutter but they won't be afraid to eat or use my bathroom.

—Mrs. Harry Wright, Salesville, Arkansas
Crossings member

Jesus loves me! This I know,
For the Bible tells me so;
Little ones to Him belong,
They are weak but He is strong.
Yes, Jesus loves me!
Yes, Jesus loves me!
Yes, Jesus loves me!
The Bible tells me so.
　　　　　—Anna Bartlett Warner

Lord, please help me to remember to treat my children as You treat me...with love, grace, and lots of mercy. Help me not to nag them but to remember that when I ask Your forgiveness.... You forgive without reminding me ten times of my wrongdoing. You even choose to put it behind You and remember no more.

—Gigi Graham Tchividjian

_____

_____

_____

_____

_____

_____

_____

_____

_____

_____

_____

_____

_____

_____

࿓

Forgiveness that extends outward to others begins inwardly, in the heart. It begins with comprehending how deeply we ourselves need to be forgiven.

—Penelope Stokes

Resurrection Cookies

Read the whole recipe before beginning....Try to do together on the night before Easter Sunday.

1 cup whole pecans
3 egg whites
1 cup sugar
1 tsp. vinegar
pinch of salt

You will also need: a wooden spoon, a Bible, a zipper baggie, tape

1. Preheat oven to 300° F.
2. Place pecans in the zipper baggie and let children beat them with the wooden spoon to break into small pieces. Explain that after Jesus was arrested, he was beaten by the Roman soldiers. Read John 19:1-3.
3. Let children smell the vinegar. Put 1 tsp. vinegar into mixing bowl. Explain that when Jesus was thirsty on the cross, He was given vinegar to drink. Read John 19: 28-30.
4. Add egg whites to the vinegar. Eggs represent life. Explain that Jesus gave His life to give us life. Read John 10:10-11.
5. Sprinkle a little salt into each child's hand. Let them taste it and brush the rest into the bowl. Explain that this represents the salty tears shed by Jesus' followers and the bitterness of our own sin. Read Luke 23:27.
6. So far the ingredients are not very appetizing. Add 1 cup sugar. Explain that the sweetest part of the story is that Jesus died because he loves us. He wants us to know and belong to Him. Read Psalm 34:8 and John 3:16.
7. Beat with a mixer on high speed for 11 to 15 minutes, until stiff peaks are formed. Explain that the color white represents the purity in God's eyes of those whose sins have been cleansed by Jesus. Read Isaiah 1:18 and John 3:1-3.
8. Fold in broken nuts. Drop by spoonfuls onto waxed paper–covered cookie sheet. Explain that each mound represents the ocky tomb where Jesus' body was laid. Put cookie sheet in oven. Close the door and turn the oven OFF. Give each child a piece of the tape and seal the oven door. Explain that Jesus' tomb was sealed. Read Matt. 27:65-66.
9. GO TO BED! Explain to the children that they may feel sad to leave the cookies in the oven overnight. Jesus' followers were in despair when the tomb was sealed. Read John 16:20 and 22.
10. On Resurrection morning, open the oven and give everyone a cookie! Notice the cracked surface and take a bite. The cookies are hollow! On the first Resurrection day, Jesus' followers were amazed to find the tomb open and empty. Read Matt. 28: 1-9.

✄ Forgiveness ✄

Satan, when tempting someone, says that sin isn't very bad, isn't very big, and isn't very important. But after the person has yielded to temptation and sinned, and has begun to think about asking God's forgiveness, then Satan reverses his field. And to his victim Satan declares that sin is so big, so bad, and so awful that asking forgiveness will hardly suffice.

—John R.W. Stott

ॐ

Forgiveness is not an occasional act, it is a permanent attitude.
—Martin Luther King Jr.

Member To Member

Last year on Easter morning, I got up at 4 AM and went to each of my siblings' houses and to my mother's house and left a gift for each person, together with a card. I wrote this message in each card: "Rejoice, the Lord is risen! My hope is that this surprise will remind you of the surprise the Marys felt when they came to Jesus' tomb almost two thousand years ago. What a gift that was!" It made me feel so good to share my Lord with my family that day. Family can be the most difficult to witness to and this way reminds us all what Easter is really all about.

—Judy Ethel, Tulsa, Oklahoma
Crossings member

_____

_____

_____

_____

_____

_____

_____

_____

_____

_____

_____

~

Why should we hold on to the sins of others while our own sins have been cast into the depths of the sea?

—Corrie ten Boom

> Lord, thank You for becoming our Brother. I ask that You would free those in prison from the bondage of their shame and disgrace. Let them see prison as a time to share in the sufferings of their brothers—and to know that You share those pains as well.
>
> —Charles Colson

_____

_____

_____

_____

_____

_____

_____

_____

_____

_____

_____

_____

_____

_____

_____

⌁

The resurrection never becomes a fact of experience until the risen Lord lives in the heart of the believer.

—Peter Marshall

> *Tomb, thou shalt not hold Him longer;*
> *Death is strong but Life is stronger;*
> *Stronger than the dark, the light;*
> *Stronger than the wrong, the right;*
> *Faith and Hope triumphant say*
> *Christ will rise on Easter Day.*
> —Phillips Brooks

ॐ

People need loving the most when they deserve it the least.
—John Harrigan

A few years ago, I decided to prepare for Easter by "giving up something" for Lent, which I had never done before. I chose to "give up" praying for myself and my own needs, and rather to focus my prayers on the concerns of others. During those forty days I experienced a new, profound sense of confidence in God's care, and my prayer life was greatly enriched.

—Mrs. Robert Steinbarger, Forest Hills, New York
Crossings member

_____

_____

_____

_____

_____

_____

_____

_____

_____

_____

_____

_____

ֆ

Humanity is never so beautiful as when praying for forgiveness,
or else forgiving another.

—Jean Paul Richter

Reading List

Feeling Guilty, Finding Grace, Larry K. Weeden, Vine Books

Forgive and Forget, Lewis Smedes, Harper San Francisco

The Gift of Forgiveness, Charles Stanley, Thomas Nelson Publishers

The Hiding Place, Corrie ten Boom, Chosen Books

Little Girl Lost, Leisha Joseph, Doubleday

Passing by Samaria, Sharon Elwell Foster, Multnomah Publishers

The Road to Forgiveness, William & Cindy Griffiths, Thomas Nelson
  Publishers

Some Wildflower in My Heart, Jamie Langston Turner, Bethany
  House Publishers

What's So Amazing about Grace, Philip Yancey, Zondervan
  Publishing House

Praying
the Scriptures

PRAYING THE SCRIPTURES
BY DAVID AND HEATHER KOPP

Her name is Terry. You've been friends since you were born. You still have lunch together, shop together, laugh and cry together. And when Terry has a problem, she still calls, asking for your help or confiding in you her hopes and fears.

There's just one problem. Terry never seems to hear what you say back to her.

Some time ago, thinking it might help if you wrote to her instead, you began to send her letters—encouraging notes packed with truth and insight, revealing looks at your own heart, honest words about the depth of your loyalty and affection for her. Strangely, that approach hasn't helped much either. In fact, she doesn't seem to remember anything you wrote. And now this latest—Terry's on the phone asking tearfully if you really love her, whether you are truly on her side or not!

Could it be that this is how God feels about His friendship with you?

If you think of prayer as an ongoing conversation between two interested parties, you could think of the Bible as God's recorded end of the conversation. When we neglect to bring Scripture into our prayer conversation, we struggle needlessly with doubts about God's intentions toward us, simply because we haven't read, believed, or remembered His love letter to us.

Every day, we face crises small and large. In the face of them, we often lack faith, asking God repeatedly for what He has already promised. Or we ramble and whine—and sometimes give up altogether. At these times, the Bible can help us find more meaningful and effective expressions for this holy conversation, and can rescue us from some of our limitations.

As we acknowledge and agree with God's truth, real conversation replaces venting. Our fixations with what we want drop away as in their place a relationship unfolds.

"Sounds great," you say. "But isn't this just adding more work?"

Not really. In fact, praying the Bible is almost as easy as opening it.

THE BIBLE, GOD'S PRAYER BOOK

The Bible is a ready-made prayer book for God's family—and the key to a two-way conversation with our Father and Friend. We "pray the Bible" when we use passages of Scripture to form prayers, or when we say the verses directly back to God, making them our own petitions. Jesus said, "If you remain in me and my words remain in you, ask whatever you wish, and it will be given you" (John 15:7). Whenever we speak to God with the words of God, we move closer to the kind of vital, effective prayer life we long for.

Praying the Bible is as old as the Bible itself. Jesus often used Scripture in His prayers for Himself and His disciples. Throughout the Bible, we see examples of godly men and women incorporating God's promises and commands in their petitions to Him. They used the Word in their prayers for encouragement, calling to mind who God is and what He has done.

Jesus and His disciples sang the Psalms together as part of morning and evening prayers. And at the moment of His greatest agony on the cross, Jesus cried out the words of a Psalm: "My God, my God, why have you forsaken me?" (Ps. 22:1).

Since the time of Christ, Christians throughout the world have used the book of Psalms as an unofficial prayer book for the church. Prayer books designated for public worship contain some of our most enduring examples of Scripture-based prayers. For example, "The Great Thanksgiving," from *The Book of Common Prayer*, is taken from Rom. 12:1–2: "And here we offer and present unto thee, O Lord, ourselves, our souls and bodies, to be a reasonable, holy, and living sacrifice unto thee."

WAYS TO PRAY SCRIPTURE

Praying Psalms and other Bible prayers is the natural place for us to start praying Scripture. But that's just a beginning. For example, we can:

- Personalize a Bible prayer: "O Father, please help me to forgive those who have hurt me, who have sinned against me somehow. I know that only then do I have the right to ask you to forgive my sins against You." (Praying the Lord's Prayer, "Forgive us our sins, as we also have forgiven those who sin against us," Matt. 6:5–15.)
- Personalize a Bible promise: "Lord, You live in a high and holy place, but also with the person who is contrite and lowly in spirit (Isa. 57:15). Thank you. Show me anything in my heart or life that grieves You. Your gracious presence is all I need."
- Personalize a Bible story: "Dear Lord Jesus, because You stayed up late into the night to answer questions from one seeking soul who couldn't grasp what 'born again' could possibly mean, but wanted to…I pray today for the ones I know who need so desperately to be saved." (Praying from the story of Nicodemus, John 3.)

- Receive a Bible statement as a response from God: "Lord, how can I, all human, converse with God—all Spirit, all power, all knowledge, all good?" *Draw near to God and he will draw near to you* (James 4:8).
- Personalize a Bible truth as a meditation: "I am always welcome in my Father's presence today—no matter what!" (Heb.10:19–22).

THE GREATEST INVITATION

When you accept God's invitation to pray with His Word in mind, you might be surprised to discover how much changes. Not only do we have a very real advantage of renewed spiritual strength, but you'll also benefit from a deepened friendship. Repeatedly and gently, you'll be reminded of God's love for you. You'll hear His gentle voice of wisdom for old problems. And you'll find that much of the lament that is a natural part of honest prayer is turned to praise and peace in the light of the truths you have taken to heart.

On this journey of prayer, we never pray alone. We are actually joining with Christ in His greatest work in heaven today. He, too, stands before the Father interceding for His children—us! (Rom. 8:34), and He gives us His Spirit to help us as we pray (Rom. 8:26, 27).

When you think about it, the opportunity to pray is an amazing invitation from the One who loves us most.

❦

DAVID KOPP *is senior editor of* Christian Parenting Today. HEATHER HARPHAM KOPP *is former editor of* Virtue Magazine. *Together and separately they have penned more than 15 books, including* Praying the Bible for Your Life, Praying the Bible for Your Marriage, *and* Praying the Bible for your Children.

The National Day of Prayer is observed this month. Pray with Crossings for local and national leaders—for wisdom in their decisions and integrity in their actions.

Scripture memorized can come to mind when you do not have your Bible with you—on sleepless nights, when driving a car, traveling, when having to make an instantaneous important decision. It comforts, guides, corrects, encourages—all we need is there. Memorize as much as you can.

—Billy Graham

∽

Your words were found and I ate them and Your words became for me a joy and the delight of my heart.

—Jer. 15:16

The Lord's Prayer
Our Father which art in heaven,
Hallowed be Thy name.
Thy kingdom come.
Thy will be done
in earth, as it is in heaven.
Give us this day our daily bread.
And forgive us our debts,
as we forgive our debtors.
And lead us not into temptation,
but deliver us from evil:
For thine is the kingdom, the power,
and the glory, forever. Amen
    —Matt. 6:9–13 (KJV)

❧
The Lord's Prayer may be committed to memory quickly,
but it is slowly learnt by heart.
—Frederick Denison Maurice

Member To Member

Take fifteen minutes to pick up loose items around the house just before you go to bed and you will feel much better when you get up in the morning. Also, make your bed first thing in the morning and everything looks better.

—Judy Wyles, Pecos, Texas
Crossings member

91

Search me, O God, and know my heart;
test me and know my anxious thoughts.
See if there is any offensive way in me,
and lead me in the way everlasting.
—Ps. 139:23, 24

> *In order to make it genuine and valid, our whole life must be the extension, the image, and the fulfillment of our prayer, and on that account there is nothing more effective than to pray in proportion to our faith. It is only if we have asked for a long time beforehand that His will be done that we will have the strength to do the will of God and help see that it is done everywhere.*
>
> —Louis Evely

❧

Jesus runs in front of me to show the way, by my side to pick me up, and behind me to encourage me.

—Charles Stanley

O God, you are my God, earnestly I seek You; my soul thirsts for You, and my body longs for You, in a dry and weary land where there is no water. I have seen You in the sanctuary and beheld Your power and Your glory. Because Your love is better than life, my lips will glorify You. I will praise You as long as I live, and in Your name I will lift up my hands.

—Ps. 63

—— *Member To Member* ——

When my son David was about five, his Grandpa came for a visit. One Sunday we went to church, and Grandpa stayed home. In Sunday School, David was learning that when we ask God for things, we ask and claim them "in the name of Jesus." When we came home from church, Grandpa and David were talking, and for some reason David asked Grandpa for money. I overheard Grandpa saying, "Well, David, now what's the magic word?" To which David immediately replied, "In the name of Jesus, give me the money!"

—Dottie Siders, Woodbine, Maryland
Crossings member

_____

_____

_____

_____

_____

_____

_____

_____

_____

And I pray that you, being rooted and established in love, may have power, together with all the saints, to grasp how wide and long and high and deep is the love of Christ, and to know this love that surpasses knowledge—that you may be filled to the measure of all the fullness of God.

—Eph. 3:17–19

_____

_____

_____

_____

_____

_____

_____

_____

_____

_____

_____

_____

_____

_____

_____

_____

❧

*The God to whom little boys say their prayers has a face
very like their mother's.*

—James M. Barrie

Praise be to the God and Father of our Lord Jesus Christ, the Father of compassion and the God of all comfort, who comforts us in all our troubles, so that we can comfort those in any trouble with the comfort we ourselves have received from God.

—2 Cor. 1:3, 4

᠅

The Bible is alive, it speaks to me; it has feet, it runs after me; it has hands, it lays hold of me.
—Martin Luther

Member To Member

𝓕 often saw my mother sitting with a cup of tea and an open Bible. Sometimes I'd come home from school to find a note in my room with a scripture verse on it and a new thought God had given her regarding that verse. One year ago for Christmas, my daughters gave me a coupon reading, "To Mom, one hour of Bible study without us bugging you." What a legacy my mom began.

—Mrs. Debbie Carpenter, Tucson, Arizona
Crossings member

Jesus replied, "If anyone loves me, he will obey my teaching. My Father will love him, and we will come to him and make our home with him.

"All this I have spoken while still with you. But the Counselor, the Holy Spirit, whom the Father will send in my name, will teach you all things and will remind you of everything I have said to you."

—John 14:23, 25–26

The Lord is my shepherd; I shall not want.
He maketh me to lie down in green pastures:
he leadeth me beside still waters.
He restoreth my soul:
he leadeth me in the paths of righteousness for his name's sake.

Yea, though I walk through the valley of the shadow of death,
I will fear no evil: for thou art with me;
thy rod and thy staff they comfort me.

Thou preparest a table before me in the presence of mine enemies:
thou anointest my head with oil;
my cup runneth over.
Surely goodness and mercy shall follow me all the days of my life:
and I will dwell in the house of the Lord forever.
—Psalm 23, (KJV)

98

∽

He is not a God far off, but one who may be witnessed and possessed.
—Margaret Fell

Reading List

The Great House of God, Max Lucado, Word Publishing

Praying the Bible for Your Life, David and Heather Kopp,
  Waterbrook Press

Praying God's Word, Beth Moore, Broadman & Holman Publishers

Praying the Scriptures, Judson Cornwall, Creation House

Praying with the Psalms. Eugene Peterson, Zondervan Publishing
  House

A Shepherd Looks at Psalm 23, Phillip Keller, Zondervan Publishing
  House

_____

_____

_____

_____

_____

_____

_____

_____

_____

_____

_____

_____

Unanswered
Prayer

UNANSWERED PRAYER
THE THORN IN YOUR SIDE
BY GERALD L. SITTSER

Stories of unanswered prayer wear down our defenses until we can no longer dismiss them as the rare exceptions we would like them to be. Each stabs us with pain, reminds us of personal experiences we would like to forget, and raises all the old questions about God's trustworthiness. Each makes us wonder if it is worth our while to pray to a God who doesn't seem to hear our prayers or, even worse, doesn't seem to want to answer them. Recently our interim pastor, Bob Mitchell, a former president of Young Life, preached a sermon in which he quoted from a letter he received forty-five years ago, in May of 1955. The letter was written by Jim Eliot, who had recently moved to Ecuador with his young wife and baby daughter to pioneer a new missionary outreach program to the Auca Indians. The Aucas lived in a remote area and were considered hostile to outsiders. Eliot expressed gladness that "the gospel is creeping a little farther out into this big no-man's land of Amazonia." He also mentioned a mutual friend and partner in ministry, Ed, who had already left to make contact with the tribe. With a sense of both excitement and foreboding, Eliot charged Bob to pray for them, especially for Ed. "There are rumors that the same tribe is scouting around there now so don't forget to pray for Ed—that the Lord will keep him alive as well as make him effective in declaring the truth about Christ."

✂ Unanswered Prayer ✂

Of course, Bob did not forget to pray for his friends. He prayed for their protection and for the success of their ministry. But several months later those courageous friends—Ed, Jim, and three others—were murdered by members of the very tribe they wanted to reach. Bob's prayer seemed to go unanswered.

I have heard similar stories, less sensational perhaps, but no less wrenching. A young Christian prays for guidance but stays stuck in the same routine, failing to get any sense of direction. A mother prays for a daughter's healing but watches helplessly as her daughter falls prey to the ravages of cancer. A faithful elder prays for victory over sin but continues to suffer defeat. An elderly couple prays for a neighbor's salvation but sees no results. It would be easy to discount such stories if these praying people were the peacetime equivalent of "foxhole Christians" who turned to God only in a panic and a pinch. But many people whose prayers go unanswered are sincere believers, prayer warriors, veteran disciples. Besides, if any of us had to prove our worthiness to God before our prayers could be answered, as if answers to prayer were a reward for a virtuous life, then none of us would dare to pray at all. Answers to prayers are not like the dessert we receive after we have cleaned the vegetables off our plates. They are gifts, gracious responses from a God who knows our frailty and hears the cries of our hearts. We pray, not to leverage our worthiness before a stern judge, but to admit our weakness before a compassionate Father.

Jesus' outrageous promises appear to be part of the problem. He has promised that if we ask, we will receive; if we seek, we will find; if we knock, the door will be opened (Luke 11:9). He taught that if we ask anything in His name, He will do it (John 14:14). Andrew Murray, who wrote the classic *With Christ in the School of Prayer*, was so sure of Jesus' promise that he believed unanswered prayer was always due to bad praying. "This is the fixed eternal law of the kingdom: if you ask and receive not, it must be because there is something amiss or wanting in the prayer. Hold on; let the Word and Spirit teach you to pray aright, but do not let go the confidence He seeks to waken: Everyone who asketh, receiveth." Jesus' promise awakens an expectation that our prayers will be answered, which leads to profound disappointment when they go unanswered. Ironically, the answers to prayer we do receive actually exacerbate the problem. If God never answered our prayers, then we would surely stop praying, dismissing prayer as silly or futile. But we have all had enough prayers answered to know that God is real, willing to meet our needs, and eager to respond to our pleas. Why does God answer some of our prayers but refuse to answer others? Does God judge our motives, weighing each request according to its polish and purity, or is God capricious, like a moody monarch? Is prayer simply a vain exercise, the spiritual equivalent of a game of make-believe? Is prayer nothing more than the haunting cry of our own voice?

I do not ask these questions as a disinterested observer. I, too, have experienced the same devastation and bewilderment of unanswered prayer. My wife, Lynda, wanted to have a big family but was unable to conceive. Every day I prayed to God that He would grant us the gift of children. My prayers were finally answered when Lynda gave birth to four healthy children in six years. She was delirious with joy and embraced the calling of motherhood with enthusiasm and confidence. I was sobered by the experience, for I suddenly realized that I would also have to help raise them. So every morning I pleaded with God to protect and bless my family.

I prayed such a prayer on the morning of September 27, 1991. But something went wrong that day. A drunken driver lost control and smashed into our minivan, killing Lynda, Diana Jane (my third-born), and my mother, who was visiting us for the weekend. To this day, I have been unable to understand what made that day different and what prevented my prayers from getting through to God. Did I commit some unpardonable sin? Did I fail to say the right words? Did God suddenly turn against me? Why, I have asked myself a thousand times, did my prayer go unanswered? I have no answer to that question. I have pondered the traditional and biblical reasons why God does not answer prayer: willful sin, trivial requests, lack of persistence, selfish motives. All of these are valid. Unanswered prayer can be our own fault, as we all know. We are well advised to search our own souls when God does not answer our prayers, daring to discover if we are shamelessly disobeying God or praying foolishly or badgering God to do our will so that we won't have to do His. Yet these explanations leave me cold, too. I believe that it is possible to abuse prayer, and I have done so myself. It is a sign of spiritual health when we dare to probe our hearts to discover if we have dishonored God in our praying. But sooner or later such introspection must stop. The problem of unanswered prayer is too complex to reduce to the simple problem of personal sin. I spent months in torment trying to figure out why God did not answer my prayer on the morning of

September 27. I finally gave up in frustration and exhaustion. Perhaps I deserved what happened. Then again, maybe I didn't. I will never know. But I do know that prayer is intended for the weak, not the strong; for sinners, not the perfect. Jesus did not commend the righteous Pharisee who used prayer as a platform to exalt himself; instead, He embraced a sinful tax collector who cried out to God for mercy.

So I am left asking the same question. Why unanswered prayer? It is a mystery to me. I find hints here and there in the Bible that point to an explanation, but I cannot find a definitive answer. The Bible proclaims boldly that God is near and wants to answer our prayers; the Bible also tells us that God can seem strangely distant at times (Ps. 88, 102). There has never been a person who prayed with greater power than Jesus; nor has there ever been a person who experienced greater agony when His Father in heaven chose not to let His cup of suffering pass. What hints, then, does the Bible provide?

First, the Bible encourages us to express our frustrations and disappointments. Nearly half the Psalms express lament, some with a great deal of emotion. Jesus had one such Psalm on his lips when he died, which illustrates the evocative power that the Psalms have. "My God, my God, why have You forsaken me?" (Psalm 22:1) Jesus did not silence Mary and Martha when they accused Him of failing them, nor did He shame them when they wept. Instead, He welcomed their complaints and wept with them. The Revelation of John promises that at the end of history God will wipe away every tear, which implies that we will shed many tears before the end comes.

Second, however distant God seems to be, Jesus urges us to pray with boldness and persistence. He commands us to pray like the woman who approaches an unrighteous judge to settle her case, refusing to take no for an answer (Luke 18:1-8), or like a desperate friend who nags a neighbor for a loaf of bread to feed a hungry guest (Luke 11:5-8). Somehow persistence itself builds faith in God, increases longing for God, focuses attention on God, and purifies motives before God. It affects us more than it affects God. God does not have to be persuaded to answer our prayers; we have to be disciplined to keep asking. We can see the importance of persistence by observing how children function with their parents. Most of their requests fade as suddenly as they appear, except in those few cases when they want something really important to them. Then they cannot take no for an answer, no matter how long it takes to get their way.

Third, Jesus reassures us that God wants to answer our prayers more than we want to ask. "Is there anyone among you who, if your child asks for a fish, will give a snake instead of a fish? Or if the child asks for an egg, will give a scorpion?" (Luke 11:11-12) God is our Father. He delights in giving gifts. He is not abusive, turning our requests into occasions to torture us. He overflows with bounty and generosity. If anything, God is so gracious that He wants to give us the best gift of all. That gift is not some cheap toy that wears out after a week of hard play. God gives us the very best; He gives us what we really need, though not always what we think we need. He sends us the Holy Spirit, which is the answer to all our prayers, even the prayers we do not think to utter. The Holy Spirit is God's greatest gift because it enables us to live life well, though our outward circumstances would tempt us to think otherwise. The Holy Spirit transforms us from within. "If you then, who are evil, know how to give good gifts to your children, how much more will the heavenly Father give the Holy Spirit to those who ask Him?" (Luke 11:13)

Finally, Jesus charges us to view life from a redemptive perspective. There is more to life than meets the eye, at least when God gets involved. He works things out for good. I think of how the story of Joseph turned out, or the story of Esther, or the story of Jesus. Could anyone have imagined that Joseph would be reconciled with his brothers, that Esther would save her people from annihilation, that Jesus, who in the eyes of His followers seemed to fail miserably as the Messiah, would save the world from sin and death? We view unanswered prayer from the perspective of our immediate experience and our limited vision. But God is doing something so great that only faith can grasp it, wait for it, and pray for it.

There is more to Bob Mitchell's story than that one ominous letter. Years later, Bob was attending an international conference for evangelists in Europe. He just happened to meet an old friend, who introduced Bob to a South American evangelist. Bob learned that the evangelist was one of the Auca Indians who had murdered the five missionaries, including Jim Eliot, who had written that letter to Bob, asking him to pray for their protection and success. Bob suddenly realized that his prayer had been mysteriously answered. The Auca Indians had become Christians. The proof was standing right before his eyes. There is no easy answer that will mitigate the difficulty of unanswered prayer. The apostle Paul prayed three times that God would remove some "thorn in the flesh" that had tormented him for years. God did not answer Paul's prayer. Instead, God did something greater. He showed Paul that His grace was sufficient for Paul's weakness, which seems like an odd way to answer prayer. It is all a mystery to me, both wonderful and terrifying. It is a mystery that draws us ever closer to God, who, in His glory and holiness and utter beauty, is the answer to all our prayers, whether silent or spoken.

GERALD SITTSER *is Professor of Religion at Whitworth College, and is the author of* A Grace Disguised: How the Soul Grows Through Loss *and* The Will of God as a Way of Life.

*P*ray this month with Crossings
for families torn by divorce—
for healing, forgiveness,
and God's peace.

According to Jesus, by far the most important thing about praying is to keep at it.... Believe Somebody is listening. Believe in miracles. That's what Jesus told the father who asked Him to heal his epileptic son....

But what about when the boy is not healed? When, listened to or not listened to, the prayer goes unanswered? Just keep praying, Jesus says. Even if the boy dies, keep on beating the path to God's door because the one thing you can be sure of is that the God you call upon will finally come, and even if He does not bring the answer you want, He will bring you Himself.

—Frederick Buechner

☞

I have lived to thank God that all my prayers have not been answered.
—Jean Ingelow

Member To Member

I carry a little pocket New Testament with me so as I stand in line (and you do that everywhere), I can take it out and read. You would be surprised how fast the line will move and the time goes by. That way I'm not standing in line fretting over the wait.

—Joan Sabella, Hollywood, Florida
Crossings member

Though the fig tree does not bud and there are no grapes on the vines, though the olive crop fails and the fields produce no food, though there are no sheep in the pen and no cattle in the stalls, yet I will rejoice in the Lord, I will be joyful in God my Savior.

—Hab. 3:19

Spirit of God, descend upon my heart;
Wean it from earth; through all its pulses move;
Stoop to my weakness, mighty as Thou art,
And make me love Thee as I ought to love.

Teach me to feel that Thou art always nigh;
Teach me the struggles of the soul to bear,
To check the rising doubt, the rebel sigh;
Teach me the patience of unanswered prayer.
—George Croly

113

ॐ
Heaven is full of answers to prayers for which no one ever bothered to ask.
—Billy Graham

Lord, make possible for me by grace what is impossible to me by nature. You know that I am not able to endure very much, and that I am downcast by the slightest difficulty. Grant that for Your sake I may come to love and desire any hardship that puts me to the test, for salvation is brought to my soul when I undergo suffering and trouble for You.

—Thomas à Kempis

✤

God never built a Christian strong enough to carry today's duties and tomorrow's anxieties piled on top of them.

—Theodore Ledyard Cuyler

Member To Member

While sending cards immediately after a loss is important, it is equally or more important to send a note a month or six weeks after the fact to let the grieved know that you care about them and that you remember their loss.

—Annie White, Orange, California
Crossings member

115

_____

_____

_____

_____

_____

_____

_____

_____

_____

_____

_____

_____

_____

_____

_____

When peace like a river attendeth my way,
When sorrows like sea billows roll—
Whatever my lot, Thou hast taught me to say:
"It is well, it is well with my soul."

—Horatio G. Spafford

─── Member To Member ───

If an item you want is over $10, wait three days. Do you need it or want it? Talk to your spouse. In three days if you still feel you need the item, purchase it, but only with cash or a check. A want should be placed on a list for gift suggestions or when you agree you have extra money budgeted for such an item.

—Joy E. Krumbiack, Bellingham, Washington
Crossings member

_____

_____

_____

_____

_____

_____

_____

_____

_____

_____

Prayer is request. The essence of request, as distinct from compulsion, is that it may or may not be granted. And if an infinitely wise Being listens to the requests of finite and foolish creatures, of course He will sometimes grant and sometimes refuse them.

—C.S. Lewis

⤳ *Unanswered Prayer* ⤳

_____

_____

_____

_____

_____

> *Set free, O Lord, my soul from all restlessness and anxiety; give me that peace and power which flow from You; keep me in all perplexities and distresses, in all fears and faithlessness; that so upheld by Your power and stayed on the rock of your faithfulness, I may through storm and stress remain in You, Christ Jesus our Lord.*
>
> —from *New Every Morning*

_____

_____

_____

_____

_____

_____

_____

_____

_____

⤳

If doing God's will is all that counts for you, then no matter what the rest of life brings, you can find joy.

—Vernon C. Lyons

> It is a fact of Christian experience
> that life is a series of troughs and
> peaks. In His efforts to get permanent
> possession of a soul, God relies on the
> troughs more than the peaks. And
> some of His special favorites have
> gone through longer and deeper
> troughs than anyone else.
>
> —Peter Marshall

ॐ

I used to ask God to help me. Then I asked if I might help Him.
I ended up by asking Him to do His work through me.

—James Hudson Taylor

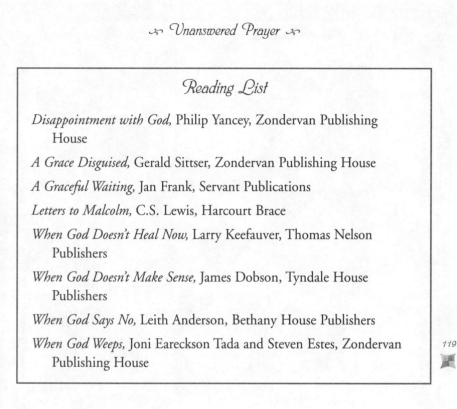

Reading List

Disappointment with God, Philip Yancey, Zondervan Publishing House

A Grace Disguised, Gerald Sittser, Zondervan Publishing House

A Graceful Waiting, Jan Frank, Servant Publications

Letters to Malcolm, C.S. Lewis, Harcourt Brace

When God Doesn't Heal Now, Larry Keefauver, Thomas Nelson Publishers

When God Doesn't Make Sense, James Dobson, Tyndale House Publishers

When God Says No, Leith Anderson, Bethany House Publishers

When God Weeps, Joni Eareckson Tada and Steven Estes, Zondervan Publishing House

Praying
Written Prayers

PRAYING WRITTEN PRAYERS:
STANDING ON THE SHOULDERS OF GIANTS
(Or, the Value of Praying Previously Owned Prayers)
BY CALVIN MILLER

Used prayers, like used cars, might better sell if we simply called them previously owned. Previously owned prayers have about them the kind of spendable currency that can be bought and sold in real conversation with God across the centuries. I, for one, like these well-used prayers, because they have already been "road tested" and proven effective in the laboratory of someone else's need. Who owned these prayers and when did they use them? They were owned by the giants of spiritual discipline in times past. Still, most of these old giants didn't consider themselves to be giants. Truly great men and women of God are blind to their greatness. They rarely see themselves as giants and often feel themselves but pygmies in their stature before the God they love.

Still, the most familiar prayers were written when these giant men and women were on some precipice of survival, studying the horizon of "why go on," and convinced that if God didn't come through right then, there would little possibility of His being God for them. Why did they write their prayers? Because precipitous times call for precision praying. There are times too desperate to allow our conversations with God to degenerate into a haphazard flow of words. Great prayers are like a last will and testament written on the deathbed; things must be sorted through, worded well, and stated unambiguously.

Further, these prayers are completely void of our own attempt to be self-serving by contriving prayers that come out spontaneously but so tightly bonded to our own egos we cannot separate which part of them is concerned with God and which part is about our own narrower needs of the moment. What surprises us is that someone else's phraseology can so instantly apply to our own spiritual need. Being human means that we, like all who write prayers, have the same needs. We all get sick and need healing just as they did. We are insecure; we feel abandonment. We, like them, have experienced loneliness, betrayal, hunger, desperation, and the fear of death. Yes, all the "giants" of the faith were simple men and women of need. Because their needs are ours, why not trust their recipes of faith.

When we need healing, why not pray this millennium-old, Celtic prayer: "Put Thy salve to my sight, Put Thy balm to my wounds, Put Thy linen robe to my skin, O Healing hand, O Son of the God of Salvation."

When we need Christ identity, let us bow our heads and pray this eight-hundred-year-old prayer of one of Christianity's most famous giants, St. Francis: "Lord make me an instrument of Thy peace…. Oh divine Master…it is in giving that we receive. It is in pardoning that we are pardoned. It is in dying that we are born to Eternal life."

When we need the all-sufficiency of Christ because our own sufficiency is in question, why not use this previously owned prayer of another giant from the nineteenth century, Horatius Bonar:

Thy Love to me, O God, Not mine, O lord to thee,
Can rid me of this dark unrest, And set my spirit free.
I bless the Christ of God, I rest on love divine.
With unfaltering lip and heart, I call this Savior mine.

Need to exalt God and remember His Godhood in your needy personhood? One of my favorite giants was Frederick W. Faber. It is not hard at all to tempt me to stand on his shoulders to gain the nearer access to heaven. Here's one of this giant's prayers that I have made into a kind of Baptist rosary. I have prayed it often enough that I now have it memorized:

They do love Thee little if at all, who do not fear Thee much,
If love is Thine attraction, Lord fear is Thy very touch.
We love Thee because Thou art so good, and because we sin.
And when we make most show of love, we tremble most within.

When I get behind in sharing my faith in Christ, I pray this prayer:

Lord, lead me to some soul today,
And teach me lord, just what to say.
Friends of Yours are lost in sin
And cannot find the way.

Feel out of touch with humanity? Here's one I learned to sing in a high school assembly fifty years ago:

If I have wounded any soul today,
If I have caused one foot to go astray,
If I have walked in my own willful way,
Dear Lord, forgive.

Writing prayers furnishes the faithful with a direct line to God; the way never gets lost by having to meander through our muddled spontaneity. So leaning on the giants of the past I have written hundreds of prayers, perhaps even thousands. Most of them I haven't kept, but I have several hundred on file. Many of mine end with an iambic couplet. Although I am no giant of the faith, I certainly consider my own prayers a planned response to my love for God. On judging others I pray:

> I must not measure others as their judge,
> Come heal my caustic soul of every grudge.

In my need to serve others in their times of great weakness, I ask:

> I want to stand in time's immensity,
> And point the needy to the Lord of history.

On my need for humility I pray:

> Rememb'ring that You died in naked shame,
> Should strip all self-importance from my name.

In addition to the prayers we might write, there are many wonderful prayers that come from the lives of saints. There are books filled with the prayers of these giants. Climb up on their shoulders in your moment of need and let them teach you why some particular saint wrote the prayer in his or her moment of need. The important thing to remember is that while spontaneous praying is every believer's right of passage to the Father, on-the-spot, made-up prayers tend to be chatty and loquacious.

Learn the grace of trusting someone else's needy prayer life to supply you with just what you need to furnish your journey. Write your own prayers; this will keep you from getting chatty in the throne room. God must have a greater fondness for terse creativity than he does rambling, run-on conversations. Seek him—at least sometimes—with precision: pray previously owned prayers until you own them yourself. Stand upon the lives of God's greatest saints, and see God as they saw him, high and lifted up. Talk to God as they talked to Him. Discover that God will hear you as He heard them and will answer you from the abundance of His love.

CALVIN MILLER *is the best-selling author of more than thirty books, including* The Singer Trilogy *and* The Book of Jesus.

*Pray this month with Crossings
for persecuted believers both at
home and abroad—for God's
protection and for the strength
to stand firm in the faith.*

_____
_____
_____
_____
_____
_____
_____
_____
_____
_____
_____
_____
_____
_____

My Lord God, I have no idea where I am going. I do not see the road ahead of me. I cannot know for certain where it will end. Nor do I really know myself, and the fact that I think I am following Your will does not mean I am actually doing so. But I believe that the desire to please You does in fact please You. And I hope I have that desire in all that I am doing.... Therefore I will trust You always though I may seem to be lost and in the shadow of death. I will not fear, for You are ever with me, and You will never leave me to face my perils alone.

—Thomas Merton

_____

_____

_____

_____

_____

_____

_____

_____

_____

_____

_____

_____

_____

_____

᪥

He who has learned how to pray has learned the greatest secret of a holy and happy life.

—William Law

> *If he shall not lose his reward who gives a cup of cold water to his thirsty neighbor, what will not be the reward for those who by putting books into the hands of those neighbors, open to them the fountains of eternal life?*
>
> —Thomas à Kempis

Lord God, almighty and everlasting Father, you have brought us in safety to this new day: Preserve us with Your mighty power, that we may not fall into sin, nor be overcome by adversity; in all we do, direct us to the fulfilling of Your purpose.

—from *The Book of Common Prayer*

I'm a single parent with one car and three daughters. We have to work out college schedules, music lessons, religious education carpools, volleyball practice and games, band rehearsals, student government, and various other activities. It's a workable arrangement—IF we can keep it all straight! The solution? A large write-and-wipe board, divided into Sunday through Saturday columns with a row for each family member. Activities for each person are written down and a separate color is used if a ride is necessary. It lets the rest of us know who will be here for supper, how we can work out rides, and keeps us from forgetting the important events.

—Susan Zivich, Munster, Indiana
Crossings member

We thank Thee, Lord, for the glory of the late days and the excellent face of Thy sun. We thank Thee for good news received. We thank Thee for the pleasures we have enjoyed and for those we have been able to confer. And now, when the clouds gather and the rain impends over the forest and our house, permit us not to be cast down; let us not lose the savour of past mercies and past pleasures; but, like the voice of a bird singing in the rain, let grateful memory survive in the hour of darkness. If there be in front of us any painful duty, strengthen us with the grace of courage; if any act of mercy, teach us tenderness and patience.

—Robert Louis Stevenson

O Lord, support us all the day long, until the shadows lengthen, and the evening comes, and the busy world is hushed, and the fever of life is over, and our work is done. Then in Thy mercy, grant us a safe lodging, and a holy rest, and peace at the last.

—from *The Book of Common Prayer*

> Do all the good you can
> By all the means you can,
> In all the ways you can,
> In all the places you can,
> At all the times you can,
> To all the people you can,
> As long as ever you can.
> —John Wesley

> The foxes have holes, the birds of the air have nests, but You had nowhere to lay Your head, O Lord. And yet You were a hiding place where the sinner could flee. Today You are still such a hiding place, and I flee to You. I hide myself under Your wings, and Your wings cover the multitude of my sins.
> —Søren Kierkegaard

> O Lord, my heart is all a prayer,
> But it is silent unto Thee;
> I am too tired to look for words,
> I rest upon Thy sympathy
> To understand when I am dumb;
> And well I know Thou hearest me.
>
> I know Thou hearest me because
> A quiet peace comes down to me,
> And fills the places where before
> Weak thoughts were wandering wearily;
> And deep within me it is calm,
> Though waves are tossing outwardly.
>
> —Amy Carmichael

ം

We pray because we are made for prayer, and God draws us out by breathing Himself in.

—Peter Taylor Forsyth

> *Almighty and most merciful Father…we have left undone those things which we ought to have done, and we have done those things which we ought not to have done…. But Thou, O Lord, have mercy upon us, miserable offenders; spare Thou them, O God, which confess their faults; restore Thou them which are penitent, according to Thy promises declared unto mankind in Christ Jesus our Lord. And grant, O most merciful Father, for His sake, that we may hereafter live a godly, righteous, and sober life, to the glory of Thy holy Name.*
>
> —from *The Book of Common Prayer*

_____

_____

_____

_____

_____

_____

_____

_____

_____

_____

_____

✧

Prayer, Christian prayer, is the supreme weapon in the struggle in which we are called to take part.

—Louis Bouyer

O God, I love Thee, I love Thee—
Not out of hope of heaven for me
Nor fearing not to love and be
In the everlasting burning.
Thou, Thou, my Jesus, after me
Didst reach Thine arms out dying,
For my sake sufferedst nails and lance,
Mocked and marred countenance,
Sorrows passing number,
Sweat and care and cumber,
Yea and death, and this for me,
And Thou couldst see me sinning:
Then I, why should I not love Thee,
Jesu so much in love with me?
                    —Gerard Manley Hopkins

Member To Member

I have found keeping a journal to be of tremendous value. I have a section in my journal where I copy prayers that have been penned by Christian writers which have been especially meaningful to me, a section where I record Scriptures that have spoken to me, a section where I record Psalms and prayers of praise, and another where I list particularly heavy prayer burdens. I am encouraged as I look them over and am reminded of how God has been so faithful in answering.

—Janice Cunningham, Port Orange, Florida
Crossings member

_____

_____

_____

_____

_____

_____

O Lord, give us grace, we beseech Thee, to hear and obey Thy voice which saith to every one of us, "This is the way, walk ye in it." Nevertheless, let us not hear it behind us saying, "This is the way;" but rather before us saying, "Follow me." When Thou puttest us forth, go before us; when the way is too great for us, carry us; in the darkness of death, comfort us; in the day of resurrection, satisfy us.

—Christina Rossetti

Reading List

Answering God, Eugene Peterson, Harper Collins Publishing

The Book of Common Prayer, Oxford University Press

A Diary of Private Prayer, John Baillie, Simon & Schuster

The Doubleday Prayer Collection, Mary Batchelor, ed., Doubleday

A Dwelling Place Within, St. Francis, Servant Publications

The HarperCollins Book of Prayer, edited by Robert Van Dy Weyer, HarperCollins Publishers

Morning and Evening, Charles Spurgeon, Thomas Nelson Publishers

NIV Classics Devotional Bible, Zondervan Publishing House

A Prayer Book for Spiritual Friends—Partners in Prayer, Madeleine L'Engle and Luci Shaw, Harold Shaw Publishers

Prayers Written at Valima, Robert Louis Stevenson, Concordia Publishing

Unchained Soul, Calvin Miller, Bethany House Publishers

Prayer as a Pathway to Intimacy with God

PRAYER AS A PATHWAY TO INTIMACY WITH GOD
BY JONI EARECKSON TADA

Rush here, rush there.... My friend Judy was steering me in my wheelchair
through thick Christmas crowds at the mall. Much to our dismay, the
chair's batteries had just died. Judy was huffin' and puffin' past the shoppers
as she pushed, then halted short of someone's shins. Finally she panted,
"I can't push this heavy thing anymore. What if I park you by Crabtree &
Evelyn while I go pick up our packages?"

"No problem," I nodded. She disappeared into the crowd of shoppers
while I waited. In the midst of pandemonium, I did what I always do.
I waited and sat still. Very still.

It's a fact of life. Because I'm paralyzed from the shoulders down, a
large part of me never moves. I don't run, I sit; I don't race, I wait. My
body is in constant repose. My upright, sitting-straight position is never
changing. Even when my wheels are tracking miles beneath me, I stay put.
I can be scurrying through a jam-packed schedule, doing this and that, but
a big part of me—due to my paralysis—is always quiet. Always tranquil.

That's why, if you'd seen me sitting by Crabtree & Evelyn, you
would have noticed a satisfied smile. I was thanking God for my built-in
stillness. Looking around at my harried and harassed co-shoppers, I could
appreciate my plight.

But it hasn't always been that way. My "natural" stillness used to drive me crazy. After my diving injury, I lay still for three months waiting to be moved from the intensive care unit into a regular hospital room. After more months of lying still, I was finally moved to a rehabilitation center. While in rehab, I stayed put in my wheelchair for hours outside of physical therapy, waiting my turn to go in. And in the evenings, my manufactured stillness would madden me as I sat by the door waiting for friends or family to come for a visit.

It was more frightening when I lay down at night. In bed gravity became my enemy—I was terrified of being paralyzed. At least in a wheelchair, I could flail my arms and shrug my shoulders. But in bed, I couldn't move at all except to turn my head on my pillow. My bed was an altar of affliction.

But time, prayer, and study in God's Word have a way of changing many things. And somewhere in the ensuing years, I discovered that the weakness of those claustrophobic hours was the key to God's peace and power. My enforced stillness was God's way of conforming the inside to what had happened on the outside.

Now, many years later, my bed is an altar of praise. It's the one spot on this harried planet where I always meet God in relaxed stillness. In fact, as soon as I wheel into my bedroom and see the bed covers pulled back, my mind immediately responds. It's time to be still and know more about God. It's time to pray.

It can be the same for you. When you find yourself in forced stillness—waiting in line, sitting by a hospital bed, or stuck in traffic—

instead of fidgeting and fuming, use such moments to practice stillness before God.

It's a crazy world and life speeds by at a blur, yet God is right in the middle of the craziness. And anywhere, at anytime, we may turn to Him, hear His voice, feel His hand, and catch the fragrance of heaven.

You can be still and know that He is God. And you don't have to break your neck to find out.

❧

JONI EARECKSON TADA *is the author of many inspiring bestsellers, including her autobiography,* Joni, *and is founder and president of Joni and Friends, a ministry to the disabled community. Left paralyzed by a diving accident as a teen, Joni is also an acclaimed artist, using a pencil held between her teeth to create images that glorify God.*

Pray this month with Crossings for the ministry of the local churches—for their health and strength.

> *In our meditation we ponder the chosen text on the strength of the promise that it has something utterly personal to say to us for this day and for our Christian life.*
>
> —Dietrich Bonhoeffer

❧

Christianity is not, and never has been, about finding the right combination of words! It is about encountering the living and loving God.

—Alistair McGrath

--- Member To Member ---

We read five Psalms and one chapter of Proverbs each morning. In the evening we read the Bible through for about thirty minutes. If we skip one day, it means double reading the next, so we're pretty constant in this. After an overwhelming day, it feels so good to all sit quietly (we have four foster children) and relax during Bible reading.

—Isabel Von Theumer, Floydada, Texas
Crossings member

145

"In" is the preposition of intimacy and one of the most important words in the gospel. It is later picked up by Paul and used in his famous formula "in Christ." Jesus sets us in a relationship of intimacy with Himself by which we experience the fullness of God.

–Eugene Peterson

> O Love that will not let me go,
> I rest my weary soul in Thee;
> I give Thee back the life I owe
> That in Thine ocean depths its flow
> May richer, fuller be.
> —George Matheson

❧

True holiness is learning to enjoy friendship with God.
—M.P. Horban

Pray about everything. This solves the mystery of what we should pray for. If we are abiding in Jesus, we shall ask what He wants us to ask whether we are conscious of doing so or not…. The meaning of prayer is that we recognize we are in the relationship of a child to his father. When once we realize that we can never think of anything our Father will forget, worry becomes impossible. "Let not your heart be troubled"—it is a command. Are we in the habit of constantly requesting, or continually talking to Jesus about everything? Where we go in the time of trial proves what the great underlying power in our lives is.

—Oswald Chambers

ॐ

Prayer is practical when it affects our outer conduct, but still more when it affects our inward activity.

—Maud D. Petre

> *Patience, it seems, is developed in the Christian life through two processes—delay and interruption. Neither is very attractive to goal-driven, product-oriented twentieth-century people like us. But our responses to both are based on faith. Faith in God's timing, and faith in God's priority system.*
>
> —Penelope Stokes

❦
A good laugh is as good as a prayer sometimes.
—L.M. Montgomery

Member To Member

Since I am a compulsive list maker, I decided to use this habit to improve my prayer life. I made some charts with three columns that have the headings, "People to pray for," "Problems to give to God," and "Blessings to be thankful for." I keep these charts where they are easily accessible throughout the day. It only takes a moment to write something I want to remember to pray about under the correct heading. I keep a chart on my refrigerator, a place I walk by many times every evening, so there is no way I can forget to pray.

—Veronica Free, Seagrove, North Carolina
Crossings member

Member To Member

I realized that my prayer life needed to be "jump-started" when I experienced a sudden crisis in my life. But God sent a new friend into my life who became my prayer partner. She encouraged me to pray when I didn't want to pray or didn't know how to pray.

—Judy Prince, Lakewood, Colorado
Crossings member

࿊

The more you abandon to God the care of all temporal things, the more He will take care to provide for all your wants.

—Jean Baptiste de la Salle

We usually think of a tryst as a prearranged meeting of lovers. How appropriate! The trysting prayer is our special date with God. We can be free and at ease because we are entering into the heart's true home. Our Eternal Lover lures us back regularly into His presence with anticipation and delight. It is not hard to honor this regular time of meeting, for the language of lovers is the language of waste. We are glad to waste time with God, for we are pleased with the company.

—Richard Foster

More than thirty years ago, I was in a situation where I knew no one. One of the sisters told me the best way to overcome the awkwardness was to reach out to someone else. In that way I'd help another as well as myself. It worked, and I've used her advice many times over and have met some beautiful people because of it.

—Sally Muller, Hopewell Junction, New York
Crossings member

152

_____

_____

_____

_____

_____

_____

_____

_____

_____

_____

_____

⁓

There should be, even in the busiest day, a few moments when we can close our eyes and let God possess us.

—Caryll Houselander

Reading List

15 Minutes Alone with God, Emilie Barnes, Harvest House Publishers

31 Days of Prayer, Ruth Myers, Multnomah Publishers

At Home in Mitford, Jan Karon, Penguin Books

Becoming a Woman of Prayer, Cynthia Heald, NavPress

Come Walk with Me, Carole Mayhill, Waterbrook Press

Holiness in Hidden Places, Joni Eareckson Tada, J. Countryman

Intimacy with the Almighty, Charles Swindoll, J. Countryman

A Life of Prayer, St. Teresa of Avila, Penguin Books

Too Busy Not to Pray, Bill Hybels, Intervarsity Press

The Way of a Pilgrim, translated by Helen Bacovcin, Image Books

When I'm on My Knees, Corrinee Donihue, Barbour Books

Whole Prayer, Walter Wangerin Jr., Zondervan Publishing House

Listening to God

❧ **SEPTEMBER** ❧

LISTENING TO GOD
BY ROBERT BENSON

"He was not really listening to me," said my friend, with a sort of crestfallen and distraught look on her face. She is a poet and a fellow scribbler of sentences, and we were talking about her visit with an old friend. She had sought out this person and was counting on him to help her wrestle through a difficult stretch, a stretch when no words would come. "He wasn't listening to me," she repeated softly, "he was only listening for what he was going to say next."

To listen to God requires that first we listen for God. It is not so much a practice as it is a posture. It is a way of attentive living, not simply a technique for effective praying. It is to be still somehow, in the midst of our days, and to know that God is God and is speaking all the time. "If we would," as the psalmist wrote, "but hearken to His voice." It is to take the time and effort to really listen.

To listen for God is to be prepared for God to sound, often, very much like someone that we have heard before. Someone like a friend or a sister or a spouse or a child. Someone who comes to you in joy or in sorrow, in hope or in fear. It is to hear God speak, too, in the voice of someone that we never notice, or never pay attention to, or have never seen before or since.

It is to be prepared for the voice of God to sound, sometimes, remarkably like our own voice, that secret voice that goes on inside only ourselves, that whispering voice that never sounds like any other that we hear anywhere else. The one we sometimes do not listen to for fear that we are just talking to ourselves and assigning God the credit or the blame for whatever it is that we are thinking. "To listen to you or to listen to me," said the One Who Came, "is not to hear you or me, it is to hear the One Who Sent Me."

To listen to God is to never forget that God talks to us in so many ways, and at so many levels, that it is often difficult to know what God is saying or how we ought to respond, if at all—if we should be taking notes or laughing out loud or falling on our faces in fear or what. It is to remember that prayer is about paying attention, rather than persuading God to speak. That prayer must also be about hearing what God has to say to us, rather than simply our reminding God of the things we profess to believe that God already knows. "No one has ever heard this glorious Name," wrote Theophan the Recluse, "save in stillness and quiet."

To listen for God is to remind ourselves each day, each hour, that God is everywhere, but elusively so, and that those who would hear must prepare themselves to be surprised more often than not at the ways in which God speaks. And they must be willing to take it on faith that it is indeed God who has spoken, and that they have indeed heard.

To listen for God is to somehow overcome the sort of sheepishness we feel, and rightly so, whenever we start to say to ourselves or to anyone else that we have actually heard God speak to us, even though we are reasonably convinced, or unreasonably perhaps, that we have actually been in contact with the God of All Things. It is one thing to say that we are talking to God; it is another to say that God is talking back.

I am thinking of my poet friend all the time now when I am about to pray, when I say that I am going to seek God's presence and to ask for God's counsel. I think of her to remind myself that if I want to hear God, I may have to stop simply listening for what I am going to say next.

And I think about another friend as well, one who wrote me once to say this: Being listened to is so much like being loved that it is impossible to tell the difference. And I pray that I will listen for and to God as though I really love God, and that I will indeed—as the psalmist wrote is possible, even for us—come to "know His power and presence this day if we will but listen for His voice."

ROBERT BENSON *is the author of three books on Christian living and prayer:* Between the Dreaming and the Coming True, Living Prayer, *and* Venite.

Pray with us for missions and missionaries around the world as well as those you know personally—for the meeting of their needs and for their safety.

We should accept with simplicity whatever understanding the Lord gives us; and what He doesn't we shouldn't tire ourselves over. For one word of God's will contain within itself a thousand mysteries.

—St. Teresa of Avila

჻

The value of persistent prayer is not that He will hear us... but that we will finally hear him.

—William McGill

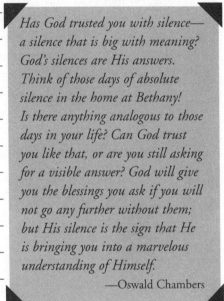

*Has God trusted you with silence—
a silence that is big with meaning?
God's silences are His answers.
Think of those days of absolute
silence in the home at Bethany!
Is there anything analogous to those
days in your life? Can God trust
you like that, or are you still asking
for a visible answer? God will give
you the blessings you ask if you will
not go any further without them;
but His silence is the sign that He
is bringing you into a marvelous
understanding of Himself.*
—Oswald Chambers

Member To Member

After scheduling events and glancing at the calendar at the beginning of the week, I am aware of what evenings (or even hours) are free and I try to keep them that way! We all need down time and scheduling that time is a necessity. I try to keep one or two evenings free and I don't even answer my phone one morning a week. The "time off" helps me to catch up if I need to or want to and prepares me to be organized in the other activities and commitments. If I don't want to catch up, the quiet time prepares me mentally to keep the hectic times in check. Do yourself a favor and schedule yourself a break!

—Linda J. Beck, Chicora, Pennsylvania
Crossings member

Listening to God

> *O God of Peace, who has taught us that in returning and rest we shall be saved, in quietness and in confidence shall be our strength; By the might of Thy Spirit lift us, we pray Thee, to Thy presence, where we may be still and know that Thou art God.*
>
> —from *The Book of Common Prayer*

_____

_____

_____

_____

_____

_____

163

_____

_____

_____

_____

_____

_____

_____

_____

Get into the habit of saying, 'Speak, Lord,' and life will become a romance.

—Oswald Chambers

> *To recognize the word of God in our own lives, then, it behooves us to know His language as recorded in the Bible. We must learn Scripture in order to distinguish God's voice from say, the voice of our own yearnings!*
>
> —Walter Wangerin Jr.

ॐ

We need to find God and He cannot be found in noise and restlessness. God is the friend of silence...the more we receive in silent prayer, the more we can give in our active life.

—Mother Teresa

Member To Member

Early in my walk with God, I was taught to personalize and pray the Scriptures. One of my favorites is Ps. 91. It starts by reminding me of my commitment to God, then moves to His care for me and His promises. It ends (verses 14–16) with God speaking to me personally. I read it slowly and thoughtfully, and by the end of the Psalm, I have no trouble continuing in prayer.

—Gert Gates, Waterloo, Iowa
Crossings member

> *The Lord is good to those who wait for Him, to the soul who seeks Him. It is good that one should hope and wait quietly for the salvation of the Lord.*
>
> —Lam. 3:25–26

⌖

When you have nothing left but God, then for the first time you become aware that God is enough.

—Maude Royden

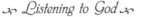

Listening to God

— *Member To Member* —

Jesse, my four-year-old grandson, was playing outside on the deck. Mosquitoes were also enjoying the evening. Jesse's mother had taught him "no plague comes nigh our dwelling." He jumped up, ran into the house, and said, "Mama, them plagues keep biting me but I told Jesus to make them leave me alone!"

—Bonnie Fletcher, Lone Grove, Oklahoma
Crossings member

Before there can be fullness there must be emptiness. Before God can fill us with Himself we must first be emptied of ourselves. It is this emptying that brings the painful disappointment and despair of self which so many persons have complained just prior to their new and radiant experience.... Complete and ungrudging obedience to the will of God is absolutely indispensable to the reception of the Spirit's anointing. As we wait before God we should reverently search the Scriptures and listen for the voice of gentle stillness to learn what our heavenly Father expects of us. Then, trusting in His enabling, we should obey to the best of our ability and understanding.

—A.W. Tozer

Member To Member

Priorities must be set, asking the Lord's help in setting them. When that has been done, see how much time must be allowed for each of those priorities, then pray for the courage to say NO to everything else and stick by it.

—Flo Crone, Lakeway, Texas
Crossings member

169

_____

_____

_____

_____

_____

_____

_____

_____

_____

_____

_____

Lord, teach me to silence my own heart that I may listen to the gentle movement of the Holy Spirit within me and sense the depths which are of God.

—Frankfurt prayer, sixteenth century

You wonder if it is a blessing or a curse to have a mind that never rests. But you would rather be a cynic than a hypocrite, so you continue to pray with one eye open and wonder: about starving children/about the power of prayer/about Christians in cancer wards....

Tough questions. Throw-in-the-towel questions. Questions the disciples must have asked in the storm. All they could see were black skies as they bounced in the battered boat. A figure came to them walking on the water. It wasn't what they expected.... They almost missed seeing the answer to their prayers.

—Max Lucado

❧

The word "listen" contains the same letters as the word "silent."

—Alfred Brendel

Reading List

God Calling, A.J. Russell, Barbour Publishing

How to Listen to God, Charles Stanley, Thomas Nelson Publishers

Listening to Prayer, Leanne Payne, Baker Book House

Living Prayer, Robert Benson, Putnam Publishing Group

The Mystery of God's Will, Charles Swindoll, Word Publishing

The Screwtape Letters, C.S. Lewis, Broadman & Holman Publishers

The Way of the Heart, Henri Nouwen, Harper Collins Publishing

When God Whispers Your Name, Max Lucado, Word Publishing

On the Power
of Prayer

ON THE POWER OF PRAYER
BY KENNETH SWANSON

Why do you pray?

What motivates you to pray?

Do you wish your prayer life were more powerful?

How you respond to the first two questions may determine the
answer to the third.

When my friend Tom Bowers became rector of St. Luke's Church in
Atlanta in 1971, it was a parish in decline. It was once a neighborhood
church surrounded by large graceful homes. But as its parishioners steadily
moved into the suburbs, these homes were converted into duplexes, then
apartments, and finally were torn down to be replaced with commercial
buildings. The streets around the church harbored dozens of homeless men
and women. "Hey," Tom said to his parishioners, "we've got to do something. We need to make a Christian witness in our neighborhood."

Well, there were plenty of naysayers, and even more doubters, but after
much wrangling and debate the parish board agreed to an experimental
lunch program. The only suitable space was their elegant parish hall,
which was set up to receive and feed more than one hundred homeless
people each weekday at noon. After a brief time, all the seats were full
at every meal. Several dozen parishioners volunteered to help out at least

one day a week. Their goals seemed to have been met, but there were still those who were disgruntled and unhappy, and their rumblings began to grow.

One Sunday, after church at the coffee hour, a group of formidable ladies cornered Tom Bowers. Quite agitated, their leader shook her finger in Tom's face as she said, "This feeding program has got to stop. It is destroying this room. It was so lovely, but now, now it's become worse than shabby. My wedding reception was held in this room. My daughter's wedding reception was held in this room. But I would never let my granddaughter have hers here. Not now. And besides that, I've seen what goes on here. It isn't accomplishing anything. It's the same people day after day. Not a single one of those people has been changed. This program is a failure."

"Madame," Tom replied, "I think you misunderstand. The objective of this ministry isn't to change them. It's to change you."

Many people wonder why their prayers lack power. If this is true for any of us, the first thing we need to examine is our motive for prayer. We often approach God in prayer as if we already know what He ought to do. If we're honest we must admit that often our prayers are to remind God, or to pester Him into doing what we think is right. Yet if we pray in order to bargain with God, to convince Him to give us what we want, then like the woman in Atlanta, we misunderstand. For the goal of Christian prayer is not to change our circumstances, but to change us. The ultimate aim of Christian prayer is for us to be drawn into such an intimate relationship with God that He shares His life with us. In that intimacy we are transformed. In that intimacy His will becomes our will. When we know His will, and make it our own, then our prayers abound with power.

God knows that we and those we care about need emotional and material security, although maybe not in the ways we think. Jesus Himself taught us this, saying, "Seek first the Kingdom of God and His righteousness, and all these things will be added unto you." In *Mere Christianity* C.S. Lewis put the same idea this way, "If you aim for heaven you get the earth thrown in, if you aim for the earth you get nothing at all." Do you want your prayers to have power? Then understand why you pray. Comprehend your motives in prayer. And if you pray in order to be open to God, to be drawn into His life, to discover His will, to be so transformed by Him that His will becomes your will, then your prayers will not lack power. Then you will be able to move mountains.

KENNETH SWANSON *is Dean and Rector of Christ Church Cathedral in Nashville, Tennessee, and author of* Uncommon Prayer, Approaching Intimacy with God.

Pray this month with Crossings for the children of our nation— particularly those who are hungry, abused, and not properly cared for.

_____

_____

_____

_____

_____

_____

_____

_____

_____

_____

_____

_____

_____

_____

_____

_____

> Our vocation is an asset to prayer,
> because our work becomes prayer. It is
> prayer in action. The artist, the novelist,
> the surgeon, the plumber, the secretary,
> the lawyer, the homemaker, the farmer,
> the teacher—all are praying by offering
> their work up to God.
> —Richard J. Foster

ℒ

*If man is man and God is God, to live without prayer is not merely
an awful thing: it is an infinitely foolish thing.*

—Phillips Brooks

I try to keep from getting overwhelmed by shopping for all out-of-town and extended family's presents early. I try to have all those presents bought, wrapped, and mailed by Thanksgiving day. Then I have the whole month of December free to just focus on my family and cards. I have the family portrait taken in October so the pictures are back by Thanksgiving. I spend the first week in December getting Christmas cards mailed, the next week finishing up immediate family presents, and the last week doing Christmas baking. This schedule, when I stick with it, really helps to make for a more relaxed and enjoyable holiday season.

—Barbara West, Jackson, Ohio
Crossings member

_____

_____

_____

_____

_____

_____

_____

_____

_____

_____

_____

_____

_____

> Holy Spirit, prompt us
> When we kneel to pray;
> Nearer come and teach us
> What we ought to say.
>
> Holy Spirit, give us
> Each a lowly mind;
> Make us more like Jesus,
> Gentle, pure, and kind.
> —W.H. Parker

ॐ

I find the doing of the will of God leaves me no time for disputing about his plans.

—George MacDonald

[One] reason I pray…is for my friends who are ill or in difficult situations. In praying for them, God always strengthens me. Prayer is powerful and I thank God for the channel of prayer. I may not have the strength to say much more to God than a simple prayer but it does not matter to Him. He wants me to approach Him in spirit and truth, which is heartfelt honesty.

—Andrea Leonard, Dexter, Maine
Crossings member

Member To Member

After attending [our church] for about three years...and still not quite fitting in...a lady my age invited me to a candle party! My husband stayed home with the kids and I met some wonderful women. The same woman was in the choir, which I had always wanted to participate in.... She told me she had a daughter willing to baby-sit during choir practice and so she also made it possible for me to join the choir. What a tremendous year of growth it has been for me and my family.

—Colleen Duncan, Coastesville, Indiana
Crossings member

> *Praying unlocks the doors of heaven and releases the power of God. God's answers are always right and good and best. Whether prayer changes our situation or not, one thing is certain: Prayer will change us!*
>
> —Billy Graham

◌

I used to ask God to help me. Then I asked if I might help Him. I ended up by asking Him to do His work through me.

—James Hudson Taylor

> We are tempted to wait to pray until
> we know how to pray. And since we'd
> rather not pray than pray poorly, we
> don't pray. Or we pray infrequently....
> But the power is not in the prayer.
> It's in the one who hears it.
>
> —Max Lucado

Member To Member

My girlfriend Kathy and I have known each other about five years. She recently presented me with a "friendship box." It was filled with goodies—herbal teas, candy, hand cream, bookmarks, note cards, and a "don't forget" memo page (since I am forgetful at times!). Each item had significance, and made a remembrance of our friendship. She also included the following poem: "Open this box and you will find/reminders of a friend who's on your mind./Its contents will comfort and cheer/until the time when we are near."

—Joan Perez, Warwick, New York
Crossings member

185

What kind of grace do you need today? Do you need housecleaning grace, job coping grace, child training grace, spending grace, caregiving grace, tithing grace, or saving grace? So, let us come boldly today to God's throne of grace, to receive His unmerited gift, excellence of power, and spiritual strength, so that we can appropriate all we need to serve Him joyfully and live an abundant life.

—Kathleen Dale Wright

--- Member To Member ---

When our daughters were old enough to learn about handling money, we gave them an allowance every two weeks. Each girl also received four small plastic jars mounted on a shelf in her room. They were labeled, "Giving to God," "Giving to Others," "Saving,"and "Fun Money." Since they learned as small children to give and save, they are good stewards of their money as adults.

—Mrs. Debbie Carpenter, Tucson, Arizona
Crossings member

ᔔ

When we are linked by the power of prayer, we hold each other's hand, as it were, while we walk along a slippery path; and so by the generous bounty of charity it comes about that the harder each one leans on the other, the more firmly we are bonded together in brotherly love.

—Gregory the Great

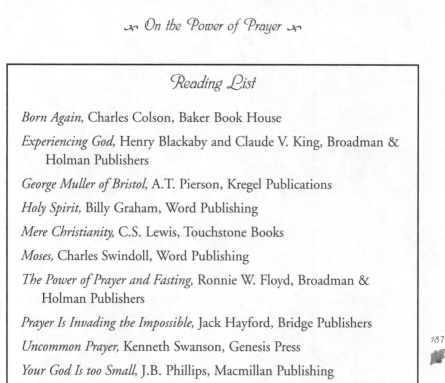

Reading List

Born Again, Charles Colson, Baker Book House

Experiencing God, Henry Blackaby and Claude V. King, Broadman & Holman Publishers

George Muller of Bristol, A.T. Pierson, Kregel Publications

Holy Spirit, Billy Graham, Word Publishing

Mere Christianity, C.S. Lewis, Touchstone Books

Moses, Charles Swindoll, Word Publishing

The Power of Prayer and Fasting, Ronnie W. Floyd, Broadman & Holman Publishers

Prayer Is Invading the Impossible, Jack Hayford, Bridge Publishers

Uncommon Prayer, Kenneth Swanson, Genesis Press

Your God Is too Small, J.B. Phillips, Macmillan Publishing

Thanksgiving

✤ NOVEMBER ✤

THANKSGIVING
BY JAMIE LANGSTON TURNER

It was a cold day in Mississippi on my tenth birthday. I was in the backyard with my sister that November afternoon. Our four tall pecan trees, perfectly situated for bases in our summer kickball games, provided spending money for my sister and me in the fall and early winter. After school and on Saturdays, the two of us would squat on the ground and toss pecans by the handfuls into brown paper bags. Our trees bore big pecans with nutmeats the size of my father's thumb.

As my sister and I scooted our way through the crunchy carpet of leaves that day, we talked of how we would spend our earnings. Betsy wanted a parakeet in the worst way, and I thought I might buy a jumbo bag of my favorite candy—red-hot fireballs. Thirty-five cents a pound was what we got at the local pecan exchange. How carefully we would watch the man place each sack on the scales, then add up the total and put the cash into our hands.

But something more immediate than our pecan money was on my mind that day as we filled our sacks. There was to be a birthday party for me that evening, and I was aglow with anticipation. First of all, there would be my favorite dish for supper. At my request, my mother had made a big pot of hot, spicy chili. And for dessert, also at my request, there would be a double-layered chocolate cake with Mother's white cooked icing. Besides the food, I had other treats in store. My grandparents were coming over to share the special night, and then, of course, there would be presents.

It's hard to say why this particular slice of time lodges in my memory, but I can close my eyes and suddenly be transported to the back yard at 629 East Walker Street in Greenville, Mississippi, on that November afternoon in 1959. After my sister and I filled our sacks with pecans, we went inside to find my grandparents there already and supper on the table. The chili was delicious, as always, and the cake was everything I had hoped for.

And then came the gifts. I remember two of them clearly. One was a dark green five-year diary, and the other was a copy of *Little Women*. The diary had a gold clasp and a tiny key, and I filled up every single page in the five years to come. The copy of *Little Women* had a glossy cover with a picture of a girl curled up on a sofa reading in an old attic. I still have the book on a shelf in my office. The front and back covers are held together with masking tape, and the pages are falling out.

I love this memory of my tenth birthday, and I return to it often. I've had forty-nine other birthdays, but this is the one I remember best. I can't even recall what I received on my most recent birthday, so how is it that I can recall the diary and book from forty years ago? I think it must be because they were gifts that contributed in a significant way to who I am today, that opened my eyes to a world I hadn't considered before, that reaffirmed for me the unique pleasures of writing and reading.

In the days and years that followed my tenth birthday, my diary and I became fast friends. In daily setting down on paper the record of my small world, I learned to be alert to life, to be specific and concise, to weigh my thoughts honestly. I saw the steady increase of my words as I added to them everyday, and I began to understand how a book might be written, a few sentences at a time with long patience. Not that I knew I was learning all this, for I was only a child. But that green diary, given to me without any idea on the part of the giver that I was to become a writer, was whispering to me every day: "Write it down!"

Little Women was the first real "grownup" novel I read, and it completely captivated me. I loved all four sisters and wanted to be all of them at once—steady and motherly Meg, bold and unpretentious Jo, gentle and good Beth, artistic and feminine Amy. Louisa May Alcott showed me the power of a writer to pick a reader up and carry him away to a different time and place. I didn't live in Mississippi in 1959 anymore. I was a member of the March family in the 1860s. When Jo got her first book published at the end of the novel, I heard another whisper: "Maybe you can do that someday."

So as we gather around our Thanksgiving table this year, I plan to thank God for the big blessings of my life, to be sure—for my salvation, for my family standing there with me, for my country, for my home, for the food spread before us. But I'm not going to stop there. I'm going to thank Him also for the small gifts He sends us before we even know we need them, before we recognize their lasting worth, before we've begun looking for signposts along the path of life. I'm going to thank Him for the blessings of a green diary and a dog-eared book.

❧

JAMIE LANGSTON TURNER *is a professor of English at Bob Jones University, and is the author of three novels, including* Some Wildflower in My Heart.

*This month, give thanks
with us for small blessings
that God showers upon us
daily—the ones we tend
to take for granted.*

It is easy to sing when we can read the notes by daylight; but he is skillful who sings when there is not a ray of light to read by, who sings from his heart. No man can make a song in the night of himself; he may attempt it, but he will find that a song in the night must be divinely inspired.... No, it is not in man's power to sing when all is adverse.... Since our Maker gives songs in the night, let us wait on Him for the music. Let us not remain songless because affliction is upon us, but tune our lips to the melody of thanksgiving.

—Charles H. Spurgeon

✦ Thanksgiving ✦

Member To Member

Our family began a tradition of making a Thanksgiving tree.
I make a large paper tree from brown paper grocery bags (trunk and
branches only). I then cut out leaves from fall-colored construction paper
and keep them in an envelope. After dinner each evening during the
month of November, the children are asked what they are thankful for
and they write it on a leaf. By Thanksgiving, the tree becomes beautifully
decorated with all our rich blessings!

—Cindy Cageao, Beaver, Pennsylvania
Crossings member

195

---

*Lord, we thank You for this place in which we dwell, for the love that
unites us, for the peace accorded us this day, for the hope with which
we expect the morrow; for the health, the work, the food and the bright
skies that make our lives delightful; for our friends in all parts of the
earth. Amen.*

—Robert Louis Stevenson

Member To Member

F keep a prayer list and then in the back of the notebook, I list answers to prayers. Because the Lord is so gracious, there are many by the time Thanksgiving rolls around. On Thanksgiving day my prayer time is spent going through the answers to prayers and thanking the Lord for each of them. It takes the focus off oneself and puts it where it belongs... thanking the Lord for His blessings.

—Norma Bledsoe, Mooresville, Indiana
Crossings member

_____

_____

_____

_____

_____

_____

_____

_____

> *Now thank we all our God,*
> *With heart and hand and voices,*
> *Who wondrous things has done,*
> *In whom His world rejoices;*
> *Who from our mother's arms*
> *Has blessed us on our way*
> *With countless gifts of love*
> *And still is ours today*
>
> —Martin Rinkart

☙

Thanksgiving is not a holiday—it is a holy way of life. It is a new
perspective that guards us from greed and self-centeredness,
that tenderizes our hearts and renews our minds.

—Penelope Stokes

_____

_____

_____

_____

_____

_____

_____

_____

_____

_____

_____

_____

_____

_____

_____

> *Remember, what makes prayer easy is not our wits or our understanding, but the tremendous agony of God in redemption. A thing is worth just what it costs. Prayer is not what it costs us, but what it cost God to enable us to pray. It cost God so much that a little child can pray. It cost God Almighty so much that anyone can pray. But it is time those of us who name His name knew the secret of the cost, and the secret is here, "My soul is exceedingly sorrowful, even unto death." Those words open the door to the autobiography of our Lord's agony.*
>
> —Oswald Chambers

─── Member To Member ───

After the food is passed around and served, [my family] plays our Thankful Game. We each take turns saying what we're thankful for, starting with the letter A and on through the alphabet. It is surprising what good things the children think of—water, fresh air, etc.

—Mrs. Bob Keene, Amboy, Washington
Crossings member

ॐ

We should spend as much time in thanking God for his benefits as we do in asking Him for them.

—Vincent de Paul

--- Member To Member ---

In 1992 we lost Daddy to leukemia, and in 1993 Mom was killed by a drunk driver. We were a devastated family, to say the least, but God has used this tragedy to bring us closer together. Our family went in together and rebuilt Dad's old lake cabin, and we put Mom's furniture, family photos, and Dad's piano in the new lake house. We don't feel lost on holidays now because we all gather at the lake on Thanksgiving and Christmas.

—Bobbi O'Neal, Sylacauga, Alabama
Crossings member

_____

_____

_____

_____

_____

_____

_____

_____

For all these smallnesses I thank You, Lord:
small children
and small needs;
small meals to cook,
small talk to heed,
and a small book
from which to read
small stories;
small hurts to heal,
small disappointments, too,
as real
as ours;
. . . . . .
What wears me out are little things:
angels minus little wings.
Forgive me, Lord,
if I have whined—
it takes so much time to keep them shined;
yet each small rub has its reward,
for they have blessed me.
—Ruth Bell Graham

On Thanksgiving day, we travel to a nearby soup kitchen to help feed the poor and hungry. It is a wonderful way to acknowledge and appreciate everything that we have to be thankful for.

—Jamie Flynn, New Canaan, Connecticut
Crossings member

ᕲ

It is always possible to be thankful for what is given rather than to complain about what is not given. One or the other becomes a habit of life.

—Elisabeth Elliot

_____

_____

_____

_____

_____

_____

_____

> *Gratitude…is a virtue we would do well to nurture. Life, after all, doesn't owe us happiness or contentment or personal fulfillment. These are not the source of gratitude, but its results. We become happy, spiritually prosperous people not because we receive what we want, but because we appreciate what we have.*
>
> —Penelope Stokes

_____

_____

_____

_____

_____

_____

_____

_____

_____

— *Member To Member* —

Our family Thanksgiving had always been a large gathering with extended family. However, one year our family ended up being by ourselves and searched for some way to still make it special. We decided that each family member (myself, my husband, and two children) would pick a favorite dish from the cookbook, be responsible for buying the necessary ingredients, and would mix and cook it all by him- or herself. Although we had a few negative responses in the beginning, we all ended up enjoying each other's company in the kitchen as well as the wonderful food. The children were especially proud of themselves for accomplishing something they had never done before. Needless to say, that Thanksgiving turned out to be a very special one and the start of a tradition we will always keep whether we stay at home by ourselves or not. Now everyone looks forward to picking that special recipe every year.

—Gay Yown, Jacksonville, Florida
Crossings member

Reading List

Extravagant Grace, Patsy Clairmont, et al., Zondervan Publishing House

God Works the Night Shift, Ron Mehl, Multnomah Publishers

Heaven, Joni Eareckson Tada, Zondervan Publishing House

In the Grip of Grace, Max Lucado, Word Publishing

Little Flowers of St. Francis of Assisi, Vintage Books

The Messianic Passover Haggadah, Barry and Steffi Rubin, Lederer Messianic Ministries

The Ragamuffin Gospel, Brennan Manning, Multnomah Publishers

Reaching Out, Henri Nouwen, Random House

A Touch of His Love, Charles Stanley, Zondervan Publishing House

_____

_____

_____

_____

_____

_____

_____

_____

~

How the Good God loves those who appreciate the value of His gifts.
—Julie Billiart

Standing on the Promises

Waiting on God

STANDING ON THE PROMISES
WAITING ON GOD
BY MICHELLE COLLINGS

Christmas is the season of promises fulfilled. The birth of Christ was the first event in God's plan to provide a Messiah for His people. Throughout His ministry, all the way to the cross, Jesus was asked repeatedly whether He was the Messiah for whom the Jews had been waiting. They had been waiting for hundreds of years.

In most of our lives, God frequently tells us to wait for Him to act. I don't know about you, but I'm pretty impatient, and waiting is not my strong suit. But it seems to be a pattern with God.

The Old Testament is filled with stories of waiting—Abraham and Sarah waiting until Sarah was ninety for the birth of their child; the Children of Israel wandering in the wilderness for forty years, waiting for God to lead them to the Promised Land. These were people that God loved—literally "the chosen people," yet He asked them to wait—with no knowledge of *when* God would fulfill his promises, just the assurance *that* He would. The story of Job is about waiting. Read almost any Psalm, and it will become clear that David did his share of waiting.

Waiting is hard. And waiting on God is usually harder than other kinds of waiting, partly because the things that we tend to wait on Him for are usually the "big" issues of our lives, and partly because we don't get e-mails or telephone calls from God. Discerning His response to our prayer is often difficult, especially if that response is anything but a great big immediate "YES"—and, at least in my life, those are rare.

Faith and waiting share many qualities. When I tire of waiting for God to work in a specific area of my life, my faith can get shaky. When I think I've waited long enough—or too long—for God to move in a particular way, then I begin to wonder, "Does He really hear me? Does He really love me? I've been waiting so long without even a hint of an answer. I've been patient up until now, but this is getting ridiculous!"

I especially felt that way about my desire to marry. In my twenties, I watched most of my friends and acquaintances get married and start families. In my thirties, there were fewer weddings, and also fewer of us "never married" singles. Then I hit forty. By this time, I had been praying for nearly twenty years that God would allow me to meet and marry a Christian man. God might have eternity, but my time is limited! Why didn't he answer me? Or was his answer "no"? God had promised that "the effectual, fervent prayer of a righteous man availeth much." He had also promised His peace that passes understanding and that all things do work together for good to those who love Him. So where did that leave me?

Then one day it occurred to me that God had said "no" to Jesus when He prayed at Gethsemane that the cup of His own death would be taken away from Him. He ended his prayer with, "not my will, but Thine." And God said "No." I imagine that He said "No, but I love you, Son. Do this for me. I have my reasons." If God could say no to Jesus, then He could certainly say to me, "No, daughter, but I love you. Trust me. I have my reasons."

From that moment on, the sense of urgency and upset that I'd felt for so long was gone. I still wanted the desire of my heart, but I could live without it. There is a happy ending to this story. Months after my "epiphany," I met a wonderful Christian man—when I least expected it. Two years later we were married, and I can honestly say that my husband is God's present to me.

God's timing is different than ours. It seems that usually He is not in as much of a hurry as we are. And sometimes he does say, "No, but I love you, child. Trust me." And that is the bottom line. Obviously, waiting has value. If it didn't, I don't believe that God would have imposed it on His people since the beginning of time. The task for us, I think, is to learn how to wait with confidence in God's grace and goodness.

If we pray and wait on God, confident that He will not let us stumble or fall, and that He loves us, then the wait can become less of a torture and more of an adventure. The verse that has always comforted me in my times of deepest anxiety or distress is Jer. 29:11: "For I know the plans I have for you, saith the Lord, plans of good and not of evil, to give you a hope and a future." What a promise!

During this month, we observe both Advent and Christmas—first we wait, then we receive. If you are waiting for God to answer a pressing concern, perhaps you can offer up that waiting to Him in a sort of personal advent. Just as you know that Christmas will come, you can rest in the knowledge that God has plans to give you a hope and a future. And he *will* turn those plans for you into reality. You can stand on His promise.

MICHELLE COLLINGS *is the editor-in-chief of Crossings Book Club.*

*P*ray this month with Crossings for unbelieving friends and family—that God will bring them to the saving knowledge of Christ our Savior.

Member To Member

Each evening in December, *we talk about what we have done that day to glorify Jesus, and for each Christ-like act we make a little gold or silver "package" out of foil paper. We put these gifts in and around our crèche so that on Christmas the Babe has gifts far better than gold, frankincense, or myrrh.*

—Donna Thiboult, Calhoun, Georgia
Crossings member

_____

_____

_____

_____

_____

_____

_____

> *Lord, John Bunyan said that if you want encouragement, "entertain the promises." And, Lord, I am a mother, and I need encouragement. Help me search out Your promises, stand on them, and be joyful.*
> —Ruth Bell Graham

_____

_____

_____

_____

213

_____

_____

_____

_____

_____

_____

_____

✌

*The work of God in our lives as Christians is exactly that—
the work of God.*
—Penelope Stokes

It may seem an easy thing to wait, but it is one of the postures which a Christian soldier does not learn without years of teaching. There are hours of perplexity when the most willing spirit, anxiously desirous to serve the Lord, knows not what part to take.... Wait in prayer. Call on God, and spread the case before Him; tell Him your difficulty and plead His promise of aid.... Wait in faith. Express your unstaggering confidence in Him, for unfaithful, untrusting waiting is but an insult to the Lord. Believe that if He keeps you tarrying even till midnight, yet He will come at the right time; the vision will come and will not tarry.

—Charles Spurgeon

Member To Member

We have found that gifts given to Jesus for the following year (reading the Bible through, sending cards to shut-ins every week, etc.) have a lot more staying power and therefore cause a lot more spiritual growth than those same promises made to ourselves under the title of "New Year's Resolutions."

—Jeanne M. Ball, Pontiac, Illinois
Crossings member

✣

God is the God of promise. He keeps his word, even when that seems impossible; even when the circumstances seem to point to the opposite.

—Colin Urquhart

In reading the book of Job, I [am] comforted that Job could not simply settle for the long-accepted religious answers when they did not make sense with his experience. When the atrocities of his physical condition worsened, and the taunting of his comforters seemed never-ending, he chose to take both his experience and his questions and argue them before God. Even in the midst of his pain and confusion and despair, even under the silence of heaven, Job never trifled with the hopelessness of shutting God out.

—Verdell Davis

Member To Member

Giving of myself to help others without expecting praise is what keeps Christ the focus of my Christmas celebration.

—Betty Jean Coltraine, Harrisburg, Pennsylvania
Crossings member

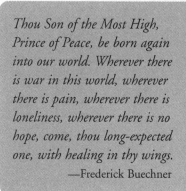

Thou Son of the Most High, Prince of Peace, be born again into our world. Wherever there is war in this world, wherever there is pain, wherever there is loneliness, wherever there is no hope, come, thou long-expected one, with healing in thy wings.

—Frederick Buechner

217

O God,
Early in the morning I cry unto You.
Help me to pray
And to think only of You.
I cannot pray alone.
In me there is darkness
But with You there is light.
I am lonely but You leave me not.
I am feeble in heart but You leave
    me not.
I am restless but with You there is
    peace.
In me there is bitterness, but with You
    there is patience;
Your ways are past understanding, but
You know the way for me
. . . .
You have granted me many blessings:
Now let me accept tribulation from
    Your hand.
You will not lay on me more than
    I can bear.
You make all things work together for
    good for Your children.
—Dietrich Bonhoeffer, written Christmas
    1943 for his fellow prisoners

--- *Member To Member* ---

My mother always baked a birthday cake for Jesus! The top layer of the cake is white, which represents the purity of Jesus. The bottom layer is chocolate (brown), to represent Jesus leaving heaven and coming to earth. A red stripe through the white cake (made with food coloring on a toothpick pulled through the cake before baking) represents the blood of Jesus; a green stripe represents eternal life. And on top, the white icing is a symbol of the sweet, wonderful love and forgiveness that Jesus offers.

—Lois Baima, Pittsburg, Kansas
Crossings member

ॐ

Jesus is the yes to every promise of God.
—William Barclay

Our family sets up the Nativity set without the Baby Jesus in it. Then we place the three wise men each in a different room every day. They are traveling. My daughter searches for the wise men each day to see how far they have traveled. On Christmas morning, Baby Jesus appears, and the wise men are still traveling until it's their time to appear at the scene.

—Sandie Femling, Vancouver, Washington
Crossings member

God gives us the Spirit not only as a seal, but as a pledge. He is God's down payment, sealing our salvation. He is also God's promise to do everything He says in His Word.

—Billy Graham

Reading List

A Christmas Longing, Joni Eareckson Tada, Multnomah Publishers

The Cost of Discipleship, Dietrich Bonhoeffer, Simon & Schuster

Hinds' Feet on High Places, Hannah Hurnard, Tyndale House Publishers

Joni, Joni Eareckson Tada, Zondervan Publishing House

Life Is Tough But God Is Faithful, Sheila Walsh, Thomas Nelson Publishers

Our Covenant God, Kay Arthur, Waterbrook Press

The Problem of Pain, C.S. Lewis, Simon & Schuster

The Wonder of Christmas, Melody Carlson, Crossway Books

You've Got to Be Kidding, I Thought This Was the Great Tribulation!, Cathy Lechner, Creation House

ANSWERED PRAYERS

～ Answered Prayers ～